Theodor Fontane

Twayne's World Authors Series
German Literature

David O'Connell, Editor
Georgia State University

TWAS 831

THEODOR FONTANE (1819–1898)

Theodor Fontane

William L. Zwiebel

College of the Holy Cross

Twayne Publishers • New York
Maxwell Macmillan Canada • Toronto
Maxwell Macmillan International • New York Oxford Singapore Sydney

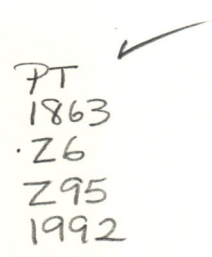

Copyright © 1992 by Twayne Publishers
All rights reserved. No part of this book may be reproduced or
transmitted in any form or by any means, electronic or
mechanical, including photocopying, recording, or by any
information storage and retrieval system, without permission
in writing from the Publisher.

Twayne Publishers
Macmillan Publishing Company
866 Third Avenue
New York, New York 10022

Maxwell Macmillan Canada, Inc.
1200 Eglinton Avenue East
Suite 200
Don Mills, Ontario M3C 3N1

Macmillan Publishing Company is part of the Maxwell Communication Group
of Companies.

Library of Congress Cataloging-in-Publication Data

Zwiebel, William L.
    Theodor Fontane / William L. Zwiebel.
       p.   cm. — (Twayne's world authors series ; TWAS 831. German
literature)
    Includes bibliographical references (p.   ) and index.
    ISBN 0-8057-8277-X
    1. Fontane, Theodor, 1819–1898—Biography. 2. Authors,
German—19th century—Biography. I. Title. II. Series: Twayne's
world authors series ; TWAS 831. III. Series: Twayne's world
authors series. German literature.
PT1863.Z6Z95   1992
833'.8—dc20   92-21861
[B]   CIP

The paper used in this publication meets the minimum requirements
of American National Standard for Information Sciences—Permanence
of Paper for Printed Library Materials. ANSI Z3948-1984. ∞™

10 9 8 7 6 5 4 3 2 1

Printed in the United States of America

Contents

Preface vii
Chronology ix

Chapter One
The Wanderer in the Second Reich   1

Chapter Two
Antiquarianism and Romantic Destiny:
Vor dem Sturm   22

Chapter Three
Balladry and Psychology: Finding the Way   29

Chapter Four
Wilhelmine Portraits: Good Prussians All   45

Chapter Five
Beyond the Reich   90

Chapter Six
Romantic Regressions: Late Morality Tales   102

Chapter Seven
Adeldämmerung: Dilemmas of a Dying Class   112

Chapter Eight
Conclusion   128

Notes and References   133
Selected Bibliography   140
Index   145

Preface

The following brief study of Theodor Fontane is intended as an introduction to the man and his fiction for a nonspecialist audience. As the nineteenth century and the Second Reich recede, Fontane has become increasingly important as the writer who has left the most indelible picture of that era. A voluminous writer, Fontane, besides authoring a dozen and a half novels and stories, devoted thousands of pages to the lore and legends of his homeland, wrote travel pictures and essays dealing with England in the 1850s and a plethora of poems, ballads and theater criticism. Considerations of space prevent me from taking up Fontane's secondary works and his literary criticism, which, although primarily of scholarly interest today, deserve a closer look for what they tell us about Germany in the latter half of the nineteenth century. Instead, I focus exclusively on the fiction, which, although not always of superior quality, is Fontane's truly significant contribution. Despite its unevenness and thematic extent, which makes even classification of Fontane's fiction a challenge, I hope to cover his most important works in reasonably satisfactory fashion.

Apart from considering several novels that have generally received short shrift from Fontane scholars, I do not break new ground in this study. I intend it primarily as an initial introduction to Fontane for those who are not familiar with the author and who may not even know German, hence the inclusion of story lines and details on publication. Obviously, for a writer as rich in nuance and poetic embellishment as was Fontane, there are abundant studies covering the entire spectrum of literary criticism, and these have become, to employ one of his most famous lines, almost "ein *zu* weites Feld" ("*too* big a subject"). The late 1960s and 1970s especially witnessed a Fontane renaissance and produced a host of important works mostly in German. I have listed a number of them in the bibliography but otherwise concentrated on works available in English. Those fluent in German will find ample scholarly bibliographies in the German secondary works listed in the bibliography, however, to continue their investigations in that language.

Fontane has been fairly extensively, if not always felicitously, translated into English. Of his most important novels, only *Der Stechlin* remains to be undertaken, and in the richness of its highly nuanced language, it stands as an Everest for any translator. More popular works such as *Effi Briest* and *Irrungen, Wirrungen* have been translated more than once. The bibliography lists those versions that are most readily available. New ones are sure to follow. All translations from German in the text, however, are entirely my own. Except for the English rendering of Frederick the Great, I have left all German names, including those of royalty, unaltered.

As is often the case in works intended as general introductions, many of the best things here are not mine, and although I have striven throughout to give credit wherever it is due, it is possible that I have slipped up here and there, for which I apologize. Of course, any substantive errors are wholly my responsibility.

Finally, I should like to thank the staff of the Dinand Library at Holy Cross College, especially Frances Sheehan of the Interlibrary Loan Department, for their assistance. My thanks also go to Professor Peter Demetz for his initial support and to my colleagues Theodor P. Fraser and Eckhard Bernstein for their valuable advice. I am especially grateful to the College of the Holy Cross for providing a Faculty Fellowship, during which much of this book was written, and, of course, to my wife, Marie, without whose support and assistance it would not have been.

Chronology

1819 Henri Théodore Fontane born 30 December in Neuruppin to Louis Henri and Emilie Labry Fontane.

1827 Moves with his family to Swinemünde on the Baltic coast.

1833 Enters vocational school in Berlin.

1836 Begins apprenticeship as a pharmacist.

1839 Publishes his first novella, *Geschwisterliebe* (Sibling love), in a Berlin literary journal.

1840 Becomes a journeyman pharmacist, training in pharmacies in Burg, Leipzig, Dresden, and Berlin over the next four years. Maintains his literary interests and participates in various literary organizations.

1843 First attends meeting of the Berlin literary group Der Tunnel über der Spree and commences friendship with Bernhard von Lepel.

1844 Begins one year of military service in the Kaiser Franz Regiment in Berlin in April. Takes first trip to England in May.

1847 Completes training as an apothecary. His parents separate.

1848 Participates in revolutionary street fighting on 18 March. Begins work as a tutor in pharmacology to the nuns at Berlin's Bethany Hospital.

1849 Relinquishing his hospital position on 30 September, Fontane becomes a free-lance writer and the Berlin correspondent for a Dresden newspaper.

1850 Marries Emilie Rouanet-Kummer on 16 October. Accepts a position in the Prussian government press office.

1851 Publishes *Gedichte* (Poems).

1852 Edits the *Deutsches Dichter-Album*. Makes second trip to England as the correspondent of the official Prussian newspaper, *Die Adler-Zeitung,* staying in London from April to September.

1854 Publishes his collected articles from England under the title *Ein Sommer in London.* Coedits *Argo: Belletristisches Jahrbuch für 1854.* Plans a novel.

1855 Begins three-and-a-half-year stay in London as press attaché of the Prussian government.

1859 Returns to Berlin in January after the fall of the Manteuffel government. Begins *Wanderungen durch die Mark Brandenburg* (Excursions through Mark Brandenburg).

1860 Publishes his collected impressions of England and Scotland, *Aus England: Jenseits des Tweed* (*Across the Tweed*). Becomes staff member of the influential conservative Prussian newspaper *Die Kreuzzeitung.*

1861 Publishes *Balladen.*

1862 Publishes first volumes of *Wanderungen,* which grow to four volumes by 1882.

1864 Journeys as correspondent to war zones during the Austro-Prussian war against Denmark for the duchies of Schleswig and Holstein.

1866 Publishes *Der Schleswig-Holsteinische Krieg im Jahre 1864* (The war for Schleswig-Holstein in 1864). Travels to battle sites of war between Austria and Prussia.

1870 Resigns from *Kreuzzeitung* and begins as theater critic for *Vossische Zeitung.* Visits battle sites during the Franco-Prussian War and is taken prisoner by the French for nearly three months. Publishes *Der deutsche Krieg von 1866* (The German war of 1866).

1871 Travels in occupied France. Publishes *Kriegsgefangen* (Prisoner of war) and *Aus den Tagen der Okkupation* (From the days of occupation).

1873 Publishes *Der Krieg gegen Frankreich* (The war against France).

1876 Is appointed secretary of Academy of Arts in Berlin. Resigns and after August returns to work on *Vor dem Sturm* (*Before the Storm*).

1878	Begins career as a writer of fiction with *Vor dem Sturm* (*Before the Storm*).
1880	Publishes *Grete Minde*.
1881	*Ellernklipp*.
1882	Publishes *L'Adultera* (*The Woman Taken in Adultery*) and the final volume of *Wanderungen durch die Mark Brandenburg*.
1883	*Schach von Wuthenow* (*A Man of Honor*).
1884	*Graf Petöfy* (Count Petöfy).
1885	*Unterm Birnbaum* (Beneath the pear tree).
1887	*Cécile*.
1888	*Irrungen, Wirrungen* (*Delusions, Confusions*).
1889	Publishes *Fünf Schlösser* (Five castles) and a third edition of *Gedichte*. Retires as theater critic for *Vossische Zeitung* at the Royal Theater, Berlin, but continues to review modern plays of the Verein Freie Bühne.
1890	*Stine* (*Stine*).
1890–91	Brings out first complete edition of stories in 12 volumes.
1891	*Quitt* (Paid in full).
1892	Publishes a fourth edition of *Gedichte* and *Unwiederbringlich* (*Beyond Recall*). Experiences a serious illness.
1893	*Frau Jenny Treibel* (*Jenny Treibel*).
1894	*Meine Kinderjahre* (My childhood years). Receives honorary doctorate from the University of Berlin.
1895	*Effi Briest* (*Effi Briest*), *Die Poggenpuhls* (*The Poggenpuhl Family*).
1897	*Der Stechlin* (The Stechlins).
1898	Publishes a fifth edition of *Gedichte* and *Von Zwanzig bis Dreißig* (*From twenty to thirty*). Dies in Berlin on 20 September.
1906	Fontane's novel *Mathilde Möhring* is published posthumously in *Die Gartenlaube*.

Chapter One
The Wanderer in the Second Reich

Although the German-speaking areas of central Europe certainly had their share of distinguished writers during the half century following Goethe's death in 1832, no novelist native to the area between the Rhine and Oder can be seen to have had more than local significance. Whether owing to the inertia of an inherently reactionary political system that held sway throughout most of the nineteenth century, or to the intellectual and spiritual stranglehold of nationalistic romanticism, German literature remained locked in a spiritualized provincialism. If they expressed themselves through the novel at all, German writers for the most part preferred to celebrate the inner person in the bildungsroman rather than to come to terms with the realities of a rapidly industrializing and urbanizing nation. It was only with Theodor Fontane, in works which began to appear early in the 1880s, that a German novelist first addressed himself exhaustively to the real world around him. With him, the German novel finally turned its back on provincial romanticism and for the first time concerned itself with the realities of urban German society. As the author of a skein of realistic stories dealing with Prussian life and values during the years of Bismarck and the emperors Wilhelm I and Wilhelm II, he stands unquestionably as the most significant German novelist between Goethe and Thomas Mann.

It is an irony that during his lifetime Fontane's fame rested primarily on his historical and patriotic poetry and on the volumes of *Wanderungen durch die Mark Brandenburg* (Excursions through Mark Brandenburg), in which with extended essays he presented a hodgepodge of history, sociology, biography, art history, geography, and the lore and legend of his native land. Indeed, the *Wanderungen* have never gone out of print, and in the wake of German reunification have enjoyed renewed popularity. Yet their interest today is primarily antiquarian. They have long since yielded pride of place to another sort of excursion, Fontane's wanderings through the world created by Bismarck, in the extraordinary novels written by him during the last two decades of a long and immensely productive life.

Fontane's immediate interest was life in the center of German power, Berlin, the capital of the newly created Second Reich. This, more than anything else, has contributed to his international reputation, for with consummate skill he presented the foibles and failings, the strengths and weaknesses, of the inhabitants of the city and of the sandy reaches of Brandenburg around it. Through Fontane's late works, the Reich in its aristocratic and bourgeois classes, as well as its hard-working and earnest lower middle class, has been preserved in a splendidly crafted literary matrix of brilliant dialogue, deftly applied symbolism and leitmotiv, and rich psychological insight.

Thus the novels focusing on Berlin have continued as living documents, works that have assured their creator of a respected place among Europe's great realist writers of the nineteenth century. The British critic S. S. Prawer, for instance, has unequivocally spoken of "Fontane's claim to be regarded as the greatest master of the conversation piece of the European novel,"[1] while Thomas Mann, whose first novel, *Buddenbrooks*, was unquestionably influenced by Fontane, declared warmly of him: "For me personally, . . . I may confess that no writer of the past or present awakens in me the sympathy and gratitude, this direct and instinctive enchantment, this immediate uplift, warmth and contentment, that I feel at every verse, every line of his letters, every snippet of dialogue."[2]

Similarly, in an essay on the fiftieth anniversary of Fontane's death in 1948, Heinrich Mann characterized Fontane's significance in even more definitive terms: "The modern novel was invented for Germany, brought into being and at the same time perfected by a Prussian, . . . Theodor Fontane. He was the first in this country who brought about the realization that a novel can be the valid and enduring document of a society, an era, and that it can shape and transmit social insight, preserving life and a sense of the present even for a much altered future. . . . In his skepticism as well as his strength of character a true novelist, in his day the only one of his class."[3]

The world captured for us by Fontane, the Second Reich—for better or worse the foundation of the Germany that exists today—endured less than half a century. Founded in January 1871, following the overwhelming victory of German arms in the Franco-Prussian War, it was forged chiefly by Prussian blood and iron through the unyielding will of one man, Otto von Bismarck. Through the latter's ingenious manipulation, numerous individual German states were welded into unity under the titular leadership of Wilhelm I, King of Prussia, who was hereafter designated German Emperor. The Hohenzollerns, Prussian kings since the early eighteenth century, now ruled the mightiest country in central Europe. From the conservative Prussian point of view, it is true, the identity of old Prussia had been swallowed by the newly created Reich. Yet that was only part of the story. In fact, a newer and larger Prussia had come into being; the values that had led over decades to the expansion of the Prussian state—loyalty, rigorous efficiency, obedience to authority, and a militaristic devotion to duty—now infused the whole empire. Despite resistance in some regions, Germany by and large became Prussianized. Government and bureaucracy were centered in Berlin, and for the most part all administrative officers, from the Reich chancellor on down, were Prussian. The *Pickelhaube,* the Prussian spiked helmet, and the Prussian eagle as well as the Prussian Iron Cross became symbols of Germany, just as Prussian values became the touchstone of German values in general.

Yet from its outset, the empire was an anachronism. In imposing order from above based on an aristocratic military elite, Bismarck had bought time for the nobility in Germany, but he could not prevent its decline. Despite an apparently feudalistic-aristocratic order, the Reich was essentially a capitalistic state. Its true leading class was not the nobility, the vestige of an outmoded military-agricultural feudalism, but the urban bourgeoisie, who provided and profited from the capital that drove its industries. Although in the wake of national victories the military ethos of the Prussian aristocracy permeated society, it was in fact the capitalist class that paid the bills and set its stamp upon it.

Nowhere was this clearer than in Berlin. As capital of the empire, but, even more important, as its industrial center, it expanded exponentially. A city of 547,000 in 1861, ten years later it had increased to 800,000. By 1875 it was just below the 1,000,000 mark and in another quarter century had doubled again. Already in the 1860s Berlin had become a banking center and the nexus of the Prussian rail network. Factories that had doubled production in the 1850s tripled it again in the ensuing decade. Necessitated by the great expansion of the city, transportation quickly shifted within the space of a generation from horse-drawn omnibuses in the 1850s to horse cars in 1865 and to Siemens' electrified streetcars in the 1880s and 1890s. By 1873 the machine works and foundry of Borsig in Berlin had built its three thousandth locomotive. The city spread itself out. Ostentatious villas and mansions were built by the rich in fashionable western suburbs such as Grunewald, while *Mietskasernen,* hastily thrown up four- or five-story apartment houses into which light or air scarcely penetrated, were left for the masses in the eastern part of the city.

Within a few decades the working classes too demanded their place in the sun, and internal strife, held at bay for a time by the chauvinism and pride inspired by the victories of the 1860s and 1870, began to threaten the survival of the Reich. At the same time, the nobility became more and more self-centered in attempting to hold its place. It is these processes—the decline of the traditional Prussian nobility, its loss of a moral as well as a social center, and its displacement by an ostentatious, shallow, and greedy bourgeoisie—that preoccupied Fontane above all. On a moral plane, his works chronicle the loss of a graceful sense of noblesse oblige through the ossification of aristocratic gentility into a rigid and self-centered militaristic authoritarianism, accompanied by gross materialism and vulgarity that rapidly spread throughout the Reich as a new class of speculators and parvenus replaced the old first families with a new hierarchy of power and money.

Childhood and Early Years

Henri Théodore (Theodor) Fontane was born on December 30, 1819, in the town of Neuruppin, northwest of Berlin, where his newly married father had set up an apothecary shop. His parents, Louis Henri Fontane (1796–1867) and Emilie Labry Fontane (1798–1869), both Berliners, took pride in being descendants of the French Protestants who had immigrated to Brandenburg at the invitation of the Electoral Prince Friedrich Wilhelm following Louis XIV's revocation of the Edict of Nantes in 1685. Possessing useful skills such as banking, jewelry making, cloth, silk, and pewter making, the Huguenots were permitted to retain their language and customs and to build schools and churches in which Calvinism was preached instead of the Lutheranism common to the region. With time, the *refugiés* assimilated into the German majority until, during the Napoleonic Wars, their privileges were abrogated. Nevertheless a sense of community prevailed well into the nineteenth century, even though, with German as a first language and French—if retained at all—as an internal argot, the *Kolonie* had long since evolved into devoted subjects of the Hohenzollern kings.

Fontane's forebears were generally craftsmen. In his paternal grandfather, however, an artistic trait manifested itself. Pierre Barthélemy

Fontane (1756–1826) became a painter and, in 1791, a drawing teacher to the children of King Friedrich Wilhelm II. Excellent French won him appointment in 1798 as private secretary to Queen Luise, wife of his former pupil, Friedrich Wilhelm III. Giving up his office in 1807 because of eye problems, he was appointed caretaker of the castle of Niederschönhausen in Berlin's suburbs. By the poet's early childhood, Pierre Barthélemy Fontane had become a thrice-married, respected and comfortable *Bürger,* and the recollection of him in his black and sulphur-yellow vest breakfasting with his third wife under his own portrait remained vivid to his grandson even in his seventies.

Fontane's father, a 17-year-old apothecary's apprentice whose patriotic zeal was "at best average" when the Wars of Liberation broke out in 1813, readily traded mortar and pestle for a musket. Home at the end of the same year after participating in a number of engagements, he completed his training. After journeyman years in Danzig and Berlin, he received his license to practice the pharmaceutical trade in 1819 and at age 23 married the eldest daughter of the silk merchant Labry.

Although sharing ethnic and cultural traditions, Fontane's parents could not have been stronger opposites, a situation that in later years caused them to live apart. From the perspective of old age, Fontane's sympathies lay unreservedly with his frivolous but amiable father, "a tall, well-built Gascon, full of *bonhomie.*" His mother he recalled as strict, practical, serious, and temperamental, "a slim, delicate, black-haired woman, with eyes like coals, energetic, unselfish and of strong character, but . . . with such great intensity of feeling that my father, half in earnest, half jokingly, loved to say of her, 'If she'd stayed in the country [France], the wars in the Cevennes would still be raging.'"[4]

Polarity characterized the geography of Fontane's boyhood as well. Until his seventh year he grew up in Neuruppin, a provincial town on the sandy plains of Brandenburg. In the spring of 1826, however, to relieve pressing debts, Louis Henri Fontane sold his shop. In the next year, the family survived in a rented dwelling, partly a slaughterhouse, recollected as a place of blood and squealing animals, while his father indulged himself at the card table when not conducting a year-long ramble throughout Prussia and Saxony in search of a new business location.

A shop was finally located in the Baltic seacoast town of Swinemünde. Fontane remembered his years there as crucial to the development of his imaginative faculties and described them in rich detail in his memoirs, while also drawing on them in a number of his novels. The town's international atmosphere seems also to have contributed to his openness to other cultures and awareness of Prussian provincialism. Obviously it was there that he began to develop a receptivity to personality through contact and observation. A case in point is the Scotsman MacDonald. A steam dredge engineer on the river, he was recollected years later in the author's memoirs as "my special benefactor" (HF III/4, 53) and reemerged in *Effi Briest (Effi Briest)* as well. It is not unlikely that he also kindled the fascination for Scotland and the Scots in the boy who was later to depict the world beyond the Tweed for his countrymen. Similarly, in Landrat von Fleming, Fontane for the first time seems to have encountered characteristics that became for him archetypical of the true Prussian nobleman, "a good old aristocratic type . . . whose aristocratic sensibility was of that quaint but fortunately more frequently occurring sort that never offends" (HF III/4, 57).

Schooling was abetted by Fontane's mother, for whom the boy read aloud from the *Brandenburgisches Kinderfreund*. Until arrangements in keeping with the family's standing could be made, Latin, French, and history were entrusted to his father, who besides being an avid newspaper and journal reader in the free time his trade afforded him, dipped into all sorts of history and geography books and popular encyclopedias. Louis Henri Fontane's talents as raconteur, as well as the range of his disorganized but vivaciously imparted knowledge and the congenial spontaneity of his "Socratic method," left indelible impressions on his son. "Not only have these stories come in useful a hundred times for me socially in my long lifetime," declared Fontane, "in my writing too they were always like a small treasure chest at hand, and whenever I might be asked to which teacher I actually felt the greatest gratitude, I would have to reply, to my father, who so to speak didn't know a thing, but who supported me infinitely more with his wealth of anecdotes on every possible topic, picked up from newspapers and journals, than all my gymnasium or vocational schoolteachers put together" (HF III/4, 121).

In 1831 the boy was sent back to his birthplace to attend the gymnasium there. Fontane recollected his school in the first volume of the *Wanderungen durch die Mark Brandenburg* as a place where the storms of adolescence had been weathered in an atmosphere of benevolence and support. At the same time, "Old Thormeyer," the much-feared director—"a colossal figure with leonine head and roar"—whose greatest claim to fame was having assaulted another pedagogue, leading to his transfer to the provincial institution, remained for him the apotheosis of Prussian narrow-mindedness, authoritarianism, and subaltern obsequiousness. In the Neuruppin gymnasium director he came face to face for the first time with the rigid authoritarianism that has become almost stereotypical as a characteristic of the Prussian educational system, an institution created to produce, above all, obedient and malleable subjects who clearly understood their duty to king and country, indeed to every form of authority. Despite Thormeyer's thunder, however, Fontane's will was not broken, and he maintained that he learned little at the school except an appreciation for institutions "of a milder observance" and a lifelong repugnance for the academic narrowness that held "that the Prussian who has been certified by passing seven exams presumably represents the flowering of mankind" (HF II/1, 191).

Potions and Poetry: Young Manhood

In the autumn of 1833 the 14-year-old took up residence in the city later closely associated with his name, the Prussian royal capital, Berlin. There he attended the recently founded von Klöden's trade school to follow his father in the pharmacist's trade. Throughout his life Fontane was by turns facetious or bitter about the trade thrust upon him. In his later days he blamed his father's egoism and squandering of the money meant for the education of his children.[5] The apothecary's shop remained for him a *Giftbude* (poison shop) and its duties nothing but *Pillendrehen* (pill rolling). Undoubtedly the lack of opportunities that a university education would have afforded him in the rigidly structured Prussian society contributed to a lowering of expectations for him throughout his life. The tradesman's need to establish himself on an economically and socially viable footing without an entré to the social levels the university would have opened for him was also in part responsible for Fontane's slow climb up the ladder of personal and professional development—apothecary, journalist, state official, independent writer, theater critic. Throughout his life he clearly felt compelled to remain tied to the bourgeois economic ethic; thus not until he was nearly 60—and even then not completely—did he find the courage to embrace the uncertain fortunes of a purely literary artist.

In Berlin the adolescent was entrusted to his father's half-brother, August. His new quarters proved even less edifying than the atmosphere at home. Uncle August, who had tried his hand at theater and art, proved a delightful contrast to old Thormayer. He also soon turned out to be a spendthrift and swindler, whose home was a place of idleness and frivolity. Thus the boy's formal education suffered. As time progressed, his scholarly zeal flagged altogether and a pattern of truancy emerged. After abandoning a short-lived goal as a botanist, the truant soon spent his afternoons where he was not likely to be found, behind the pages of literary gazettes in an out-of-the-way café on the northeast side of Berlin. Consuming theater reviews, novellas, and poetry in local newspapers and literary journals, the young Fontane whiled away hours in what proved to be his true classroom. He had fallen in love with the written word.

On 1 April 1836, Fontane entered into an apprenticeship for the trade of apothecary at the White Swan Pharmacy (Zum Weißen Schwann) in central Berlin. Its owner, Wilhelm Rose, came to typify for his apprentice the moneybag mentality of the bourgeoisie that he immortalized decades later in *Frau Jenny Treibel* (*Jenny Treibel*). Another of the traits providing ammunition for future parody was his employer's inclination "thoroughly to admire everything that came from him or belonged to him" (HF III/4, 187). Nevertheless, in Rose's pharmacy the young man was able to indulge his budding interests by dipping into the works of German literary lions such as Gutzkow, Mundt, Laube, Weinberg, and other members of the radical Young German wing of German literature he found there. Thus the apprentice Fontane received only a mild admonition when discovered one night by his master while engrossed in a leading literary journal with all gas jets in the shop ablaze. In Wilhelm Rose's establishment, he was given to know, something of that sort could indeed happen, for it was the very thing that differentiated it from the rest.

Despite a preoccupation with literature and a loathing for his teacher and the potions he was forced to prepare, Fontane completed his apprenticeship in 1839, three months before the end of the normal four-year term. Shortly thereafter, his first novella, *Geschwisterliebe* (Sibling love), appeared in the *Berliner Figaro*.[6]

Fontane's journeyman years as an apothecary were a period of painful development. Bound to the pharmacist's bench by economic necessity, he yearned to devote himself to a literary calling. His refuge from the drudgery of the shop became literary clubs such as the one dedicated to the romantic German-Hungarian poet Nickolaus Lenau, for whose works he retained a lifelong affection. Another group he frequented was devoted to the most admired German formalist, Count Platen, whose enthusiasm for the Polish Revolution also struck a sympathetic note in the young man. Above all, such literary organizations became stepping-stones for the would-be writer to circles he was not likely to reach otherwise.

Fontane also became rapidly politicized. Like many Prussians, he had greeted Friedrich Wilhelm IV's ascent to the throne as a new beginning for the country. Although his predecessor had promised a constitutional monarchy ever since the Wars of Liberation, hopes had faded that such promises would ever be realized. The policies instituted throughout Germany and Austria under the reactionary leadership of Metternich created an atmosphere of disappointment and distrust that intensified as increasingly restrictive measures were employed. The pursuit of the liberalization of Germany, formulated in the dream of a free, democratic and unified nation, was centered primarily in academic and literary circles. Thus, not only were the young pharmacist's literary interests nourished in the organizations with which he became affiliated, but throughout the 1840s they also brought him into contact with radical political ideas that strongly influenced his further development.

Journeyman duties also expanded his range of experience. After a brief stint in the small town of Burg near Magdeburg in the last months of 1840, Fontane moved on to Leipzig. The first large city other than Berlin that he had seen, the Saxon capital proved enriching; its charm revealed for him the contrasting severity of Berlin just as the easier-going ways of its inhabitants placed the provinciality of his Prussian countrymen into focus. In Leipzig he soon attached himself to the circle associated with *Die Eisenbahn* (The Railroad), a journal whose modernistic name suggested its liberal leanings. In September 1842, "Mönch und Ritter" ("Monk and knight"), a poem describing the joint tyranny of clergy and nobility, and reflective of the anticlerical leanings of the liberal movement, appeared in the paper.[7] Not surprisingly, Fontane affiliated himself in Leipzig with an organization of students, intellectuals, and political firebrands who, because of their devotion to the revolutionary ideals exemplified by such poets as Georg Herwegh, Ferdinand Freiligrath, and Heine, he later classified somewhat ironically in his memoirs as the Herwegh Club. Recent investigation has revealed that it was more than a merely literary circle. It was clearly an organization of relatively radical individuals whose devotion to protocommunism, socialism, and other radical manifestations of the liberal cause in more than one case resulted in their running afoul of the law, and in Robert Blum's case caused his execution.[8] Nor was their radical message lost on Fontane; his writing generally took on a more urgent political and social note that continued throughout the decade.

Thus, among the products of 1842 and 1843 were translations of poems by the British Anti-Corn Law poets John Critchley Prince, Robert Nicoll, and Ebenezer Elliot, now forgotten spokesmen for the downtrodden and exploited poor of England in the age of industrial expansion. Fontane's introduction to his translations shows a strong sympathy for socialism. "Is it fitting," he argued, "to stand in the way of efforts whose goal is the happiness, joy, and peace of society?"[9] Never published for various reasons, the John Prince manuscript also gives an indication of the young poet's fascination with the British scene even before his first visit to England.

By the summer of 1842 Fontane had moved on to Dresden. On completion of his journeyman year there, he stayed for a time again in Leipzig. In October 1843, however, he returned to the home of his parents, now living in the remote town of Letschin in eastern Prussia, where his father, whose gaming and financial fortunes had continued to worsen, owned a smaller shop. Working there as an assistant, the young man toyed with beginning university studies in medicine or history. But Horace and Livy as well as a translation of *Hamlet,* not to mention his pharmacist's duties, were put aside early in 1844, when he reported to the Kaiser Franz Regiment in Berlin for his obligatory year of military service.

Fontane's recollections make it evident that in the army of Friedrich Wilhelm IV, training was hardly strenuous. Drill, guard duty, and maneuvers left ample leisure for other pursuits. By and large, the literary pharmacist seems to have enjoyed his experiences in the military, experiences that endowed him with a high regard for soldiering in whatever uniform he found it. Certainly he gained insight into aspects of army life that stood him in good stead when several decades later he visited many battlefields in the capacity of reporter.

The high point of his service year had little to do with musket and bayonet, however. In *Von Zwanzig bis Dreißig* (From twenty to thirty), Fontane relates how while he was chatting with comrades, a school friend appeared out of the blue and offered to pay his expenses as a companion for two weeks in England because of his knowledge of the language. He made an appeal to his battalion commander, who advised him to make his case to the regimental colonel with equal ardor. Apparently he did so for the recruit gained two weeks' leave and set sail for England immediately.

Like most first encounters of those predisposed to appreciate, it was a memorable experience. The young Anglophile eagerly took in the bustle of Greenwich Fair, Kew, Richmond, Eton. At Windsor, he thrilled to the sight of Czar Nicholas in the company of Prince Albert, riding past after reviewing the Coldstream Guards. In the Tudor Gallery of Hampton Court, a small portrait of Mary Stuart deeply affected him. The Tower and Westminster Abbey also worked their magic on the impressionable young Prussian, who also enjoyed a glimpse into the life-style of the British gentry when Mr. Burford, a kindly Englishman at his hotel table, invited him overnight to his home outside London. There "in the hospitable English house,"[10] Fontane astonished his host and family by reciting Shakespeare and Byron and for perhaps the only time in his life yielded to the demand that he sing a German folk song. It was his first encounter with a British drawing room.

Fontane's acquaintance with Bernhard von Lepel, who had been first lieutenant in his company and who in the next decade became his closest friend, probably predates his military service.[11] Through Lepel he was introduced to the celebrated Berlin literary club Der Tunnel über der Spree (The Tunnel over the River Spree), and, while still in uniform, became a member in September 1844. As its name suggests, a humorous tone predominated at the group's creation in 1827. By Fontane's time, however, it had evolved into a society composed of individuals for whom poetry was a more serious avocation. In his memoirs, Fontane lists 57 names of members during the period of his most active participation, including public servants, lawyers, physicians, professors, and military officers, not to mention a number of artists and poets of repute in the nineteenth century. Equally important for him, however, was acquaintance with individuals who were later to foster his career as a civil servant and journalist.

Fontane remained an active participant for more than a decade, contributing poems almost weekly and rising finally to become "the worshipful chief" ("das angebetete Haupt"). Initially taken to task for violating the prohibition against political matters with his first offerings, he soon turned to a genre more in consonance with his personal inclinations and gifts and far less likely to offend the conservative leanings that prevailed in the Tunnel. It became his chief mode of expression for the ensuing decade: the historical ballad.

The impact of the Tunnel on Fontane's development is not without its critics who see in its antiquarianism and conservative aestheticism a false path. Yet there can be no question of his enthusiastic commitment. Indeed the Tunnel atmosphere was so congenial to him that over the years he was instrumental in establishing several subgroupings under the headings Rütli and Elora. Through these organizations and the historic-romantic balladry they fostered, he discovered the most suitable mode of expression for his talents at this stage in his development. The subjects he treated not only conformed to what his colleagues considered serious poetry, they were also deeply congenial to his own inclinations. The stimulus he found in the English ballad through acquaintance with Sir Walter Scott and Bishop Percy combined with his inborn love of history and anecdote to produce a first artistic flourishing. The historical garb of the ballad, so alien to twentieth-century tastes but so congenial to mid-nineteenth-century Germany, was the ideal medium for Fontane's early literary expression. Nothing makes this more evident than the antiquarian interests that continued to shape the prose works that followed in the next decades—the English travel books, the *Wanderungen durch die Mark Brandenburg,* and his first novel, *Vor dem Sturm (Before the Storm)*, more than a quarter century later.

Nor was it only in literary matters that the organization had a determining influence. There can be no question that the Tunnel, as Fontane found it, was a society inherently dedicated to the status quo, and not just in poetic matters. Its aesthetic tenets were rooted in a deeply felt conservatism and suspicion towards reform of any sort, literary or social. Far from the radicals of the Herwegh Club of earlier days, its Sunday-afternoon poets were for the most part associated either directly or indirectly with the Prussian government, the nobility, or the bourgeoisie. Over time Fontane could scarcely avoid being shaped by the companionship of individuals with whom he debated literature weekly and developed personal relationships. A decade after becoming a member, he openly admitted that it was through the Tunnel that he "found himself again and once more mounted the nag" with which he put a distance between himself and his liberal views of younger days.[12]

Yet in the years immediately before 1850 he was by no means ready to ride the nag of Prussian reaction. During his early years in the Tunnel, Fontane's poetry may have taken on an essentially conservative aestheticism and in the *Preußenlieder,* a popular series of ballads devoted to Prussian historical figures, he might have come perilously close to jingoism. Yet in his letters and newspaper articles there could be no question regarding his ongoing allegiance to the revolutionary cause.[13]

When on 18 March 1848, inspired by events earlier that year in Paris, the people of Germany took to the barricades, among those swept by the tide in Berlin was the 29-year-old pharmacist-poet Fontane. His actual role is unclear. If we are to believe his memoirs, written nearly half a century after the event, his involvement seems to have been more comical than serious. From the vantage point of old age, he tended to dismiss his activities with irony and humor. Considering the actual tenor of his writings in those tumultuous times, however, it is difficult to imagine that his activities were as harmless as the elderly author chose to suggest. According to his reminiscences, after failing to ring the tocsin, Fontane found himself part of a crowd that stormed and plundered a nearby theater of any available implements of war. The embarrassed tone in which events are recounted in *Von Zwanzig bis Dreißig* notwithstanding, it strains all credulity that the former non-commissioned officer of the Kaiser Franz Infantry Regiment, but a few years out of uniform, could actually have stuffed so much powder into the carbine obtained from the theater props as to have rendered it a greater danger to himself than to the approaching troops. Similarly, whatever part he played, either on the barricades or in discussions as an elector for a representative to the Frankfurt parliament, must have been carried out with zeal and conviction. Clearly the election process was a heated and serious one and scarcely as informal as the author would have his readers believe in his memoirs, written almost 40 years later (Nürnberger, 134).

In addition to the political crisis, events in Fontane's personal life were coming to a head at this time. By the summer of 1848, he had given up his post at Jung's pharmacy; increasing notoriety as the author of inflammatory poetry, not to mention his political activities, had endeared him neither to his colleagues nor his employers. A friend of his mother obtained for him an undemanding post as the private instructor in pharmacy to several Protestant nuns at Bethany Hospital in Berlin, so that for the next year he was able to devote himself extensively to literature. Among his chief undertakings was a never-completed drama on Charles I, *Carl Stuart,* in which the contemporary

German political problem, the unwillingness of the king to heed the demands of the times, found expression in Engish costume.

Nevertheless, his personal situation began to depress him. In March 1849 Fontane learned from Dresden that he was for the second time the father of an illegitimate child. Moreover, since 1845 he had been engaged to Emilie Rouanet-Kummer, whom he had known since the days with his uncle. Marriage had been put off until a more favorable opportunity presented itself, but by 1849 the certitude that such prospects were not likely to be soon realized pressed in on him. The end of his position at Bethany intensified his hopelessness and frustration. By October 1849, a few months short of his thirtieth birthday, jobless, living in a wretched furnished room in Berlin, disgusted with the bachelor's life to which his prospects condemned him, Fontane was near despair and even considered abandoning everything to begin anew in New York. Under any circumstances, he was eager to close the book on the pharmacist's trade.

Through a friend, a position was arranged for him as Berlin correspondent of the radical socialist anti-Prussian *Dresdener Zeitung*. Although maintaining that political reporting was not his strength, Fontane accepted the offer and contributed weekly and sometimes biweekly articles describing, analyzing, and criticizing political events in the Prussian capital for the Saxon journal from mid-November 1849 to April 1850. It marked the beginning of an extended career in journalism, which became a necessary adjunct to his quest for literary laurels.

Journalist and Government Correspondent: England

Notwithstanding articles in the Dresden newspaper that called for Prussia's dissolution in order to bring about the establishment of a unified and free Germany, by early 1850 Fontane was ready to join the other political camp. No substantive documentary evidence clearly chronicles the reasons for his change of heart. How we are to reconcile the exuberant essayist of revolution with the subaltern role he played in the reactionary Manteuffel government is a question that has long vexed Fontane scholarship. Obviously he must have come to the realization, even while at work on incendiary articles for the *Dresdener Zeitung,* that the prospects for the liberal program were hopeless. Contact with conservative elements in the Tunnel probably also convinced him that there were men of honor, integrity, and discrimination who stood on the side of reaction. In addition, the recognition that a decade of striving had led nowhere, and that establishment as a pharmacist was impossible without the capital to buy a shop, not to mention the simple desire to marry and to live a comfortable middle-class existence, preferably by means of his pen, all must have contributed to the thirty-one-year-old's decision to turn to friends from the Tunnel and to seek and accept a position with the government press office—and to marry in October.

For the next half decade, with brief interruptions during which he made ends meet by tutoring in English, German, and geography as well as by occasional work as a pharmacist, Fontane worked primarily for the Literarisches Kabinett. Essentially a propaganda bureau of the Prussian government, its primary function was to create support for government policy through manipulation of the domestic and foreign press. Bitterly unhappy to be part of a system he abhorred, Fontane nevertheless persevered, recognizing that no other avenue was open to him. At the same time, England continued as a focal point in his thinking. He continued improving his English, studying British literature, and writing ballads based on British history for the Tunnel, as well as translating and evolving grandiose literary plans such as an epic devoted to Friedrich Barbarossa. In February 1852, financed by contributions from the Tunnel, his father, and the same friend who had underwritten the trip of 1844, he applied to be installed for six months as government correspondent in London. Although initially reduced to two months, his request was granted. Thus Fontane returned to London as feature writer for the conservative *Preußische Zeitung,* and remained there from late April to September 1852. Apart from improved English, acquaintance with Thackeray's *Vanity Fair,* which became a favorite book, and a more objective and critical attitude towards Britain in the heyday of early Victorian expansion and materialism, the chief result of these months was the first of his extended prose works, a collection of articles and studies on England and the English published in 1854 under the title *Ein Sommer in London* (A summer in London).

On his return to Berlin, he once more found employment with the government in what was now the Zentralstelle für Presse Angelegenheiten (Central Press Office). His duties included proofreading the *Preußische Zeitung* and reading and excerpting material relating to Prussian politics that had appeared in English newspapers. To make ends meet, he also continued as a tutor. He did not neglect poetry, however.

Fontane's first significant document of literary criticism, "Unsere lyrische und epische Poesie seit 1848" ("Our lyric and epic poetry since 1848"), in which the young writer reckoned with the obsolete model of German classicism and the recent literary past in Germany, and called for a new realism, appeared in 1853. In the same year, under his editorship the first edition of the literary annual *Argo* made its debut, a product of a subgroup of the Tunnel, the Rütli. Along with several ballads, he contributed several prose tales, "Tuch und Locke" ("Handkerchief and lock of hair"), and "James Monmouth," relatively conventional works of the era, neither of which were to see the light of day again until 1929.

In September 1855 Fontane returned to England for his third and longest visit. This time his work was intended as a corrective to the deleterious effects of liberal press agencies whose reports in German newspapers ran counter to state interests. Primarily, he was to function as a columnist from London reporting on comments in British newspapers, which, because of Prussia's neutrality in the Crimean War, had taken a distinctly anti-Prussian tone. In addition to collecting, reporting, and translating all essential parts of major British dailies with an assistant, he was required to write an interpretive covering article and get the whole thing in the mail to Germany by early afternoon for dissemination by the Central Press Agency for use in German papers several times a week. The task proved impossible. Fontane's poorly funded operation could not match the competition. Moreover, once the Crimean War ended, the situation was no longer acute. Through the good offices of his superior, however, his stay was extended. His duties were also altered to those of press attaché to the Prussian Embassy and free-lance foreign correspondent, writing feature articles, mostly on England's institutions and cultural scene, for a number of Prussian newspapers. The high point of the three-and-a-half-year stay, during which his family intermittently also resided with him, was a two-week trip to Scotland in August 1858, in the company of Lepel. Fontane's essentially literary-based itinerary is traced in the second of his travel books, *Jenseits des Tweed* (*Across the Tweed*) 1860, published a year after his return.

His sojourns in England, especially the third, did much for Fontane. His interest in the country, primarily poetic rather than political, was naturally nourished and in great measure sated. Yet observing life in the most bustling and modern state of Europe obviously endowed him with a critical eye for the highly conservative institutions and life-style of his homeland. At the same time, because of his position as a correspondent on temporary duty abroad, in the pay moreover of a foreign government, he remained essentially an outsider in England, a factor that necessarily fostered his sense of being Prussian. It was a feeling that culminated in the motto of *Wanderungen durch die Mark Brandenburg:* "Only foreign lands teach us what we possess in our homeland" (HF II/1, 9).

But there were other gains. In addition to intensifying an already remarkable industriousness and discipline that kept him at his desk for hours each day, the English visits matured his powers of observation and ability to digest and synthesize what he saw. Studying Britain in the 1850s, Fontane developed a sixth sense for social customs and values, personalities and landscapes, that served initially as the basis of his travel books, and later to enrich his novels. Moreover, as Helmuth Nürnberger (Nürnberger, 224) has pointed out, inasmuch as Victorian England was several decades ahead of Germany in socioeconomic development, Fontane evolved there an understanding of the bourgeoisie and its mores that permitted him to recognize and depict these elements even as they were taking shape in Bismarck's Reich some 20 years later.

Editor and Critic: *Wanderungen*

When in October 1858 Prince Wilhelm of Prussia became prince regent, replacing his elder brother, King Friedrich Wilhelm IV, now physically and mentally incapable of ruling, it was again believed by many that a new and more liberal era had begun for Prussia. Fontane, who had long since desired to return home, presented his case to the authorities, arguing that a warmer relationship between Prussia and England now rendered his efforts useless. His request granted, he left England forever on 15 January 1859 to return to Berlin and complete uncertainty. Association with the Manteuffel regime, which he had served loyally if without conviction for a decade, made the likelihood of employment with the new administration slim, even though its principles were more akin to his own. As was to be expected, the new directors of the Central Press Agency had no position in mind for the former English correspondent. Efforts by friends to gain him an appointment as court librarian in Bavaria came to nothing. With great reluctance, he finally took a post at the English desk of Prussia's most conservative newspaper, *Die neue Preußische Zeitung,* popularly known as *Die Kreuzzeitung* for the Iron Cross on its masthead. There he was to remain for a decade.

At the same time he was becoming a literary presence. The fruits of his Scottish excursion, *Bilder und Briefe aus Schottland* (Pictures and letters from Scotland), which in book form was titled *Jenseits des Tweed* (1860), appeared first in the highly reputed liberal daily *Die Vossische Zeitung* (Voss's News). His ballads were collected in one volume. Even more important, Fontane began to devote himself to an idea he had first conceived in England, a study of the lore and legend of his homeland. Over the years the idea expanded to the four volumes of *Wanderungen durch die Mark Brandenburg* (1862–1882), which served for most educated Germans during his lifetime, his novels notwithstanding, as the basis of his fame.

The 1860s were for Fontane a period of feverish journalistic activity in a Prussia of intense military and political turmoil. None of this was conducive to his literary development. Prussia's war of 1864, as an ally of Austria against Denmark, its war of 1866 against Austria, and the 1870–71 war against France, leading to ultimate German unification, took the journalist Fontane to numerous battlefields and ultimately resulted in three massive illustrated tomes. None proved commercially successful nor was any republished during his lifetime.[14] During this period the poet Fontane came almost to a halt, and he also temporarily abandoned work on a novel that had been in the planning stages for over a decade.

From a literary standpoint, the most valuable outcome of Fontane's preoccupation with Prussia's military adventures was the recounting of his own near fatal misadventure, *Kriegsgefangen* (Prisoner of war) (1870), a brief book describing his imprisonment as a spy from September to December 1870. Next to it stands *Aus den Tagen der Okkupation* (From the days of the occupation) (1871), a hastily written journal of a trip through occupied France in the spring of 1871. Both books reveal the author, whose powers of observation, discrimination, understanding of human nature, and tolerance were mightily extended during his eight weeks in captivity, attempting to present the defeated enemy to a chauvinistic Prussian public that was wallowing in victory and a sense of military and moral superiority. As such, they are significant stations along Fontane's own path to skeptical objectification of his homeland.

In April 1871, after a decade with a publication whose political alignment he did not share, Fontane withdrew from the *Kreuzzeitung*.

It was a bitter blow to his wife, who throughout their marriage had yearned for a comfortable and secure home and for whom the uncertainty of free-lance journalism remained a constant source of anxiety. In June, however, Fontane secured a moderately remunerative post as theater critic for the *Vossische Zeitung,* a position in which he was gradually to establish himself as one of the leading literary and cultural commentators of Wilhelmine Berlin. In his theater criticism Fontane proved a highly astute and progressive force, keenly discerning, kind yet witty, but unforgiving where he saw inferiority, and unhesitatingly smoothing the way for the new while recognizing the virtues of the old. It was not the least of his merits to recognize early the genius of such giants of late nineteenth-century theater as Ibsen and Gerhart Hauptmann.

A Novelist Is Born: The Old Fontane

In 1876, at the age of 57, Fontane obtained through well-meaning friends the position of first secretary of the Berlin Academy of Arts. The post was an opportunity to settle into the comfortably secure existence of a Prussian cultural official with the guarantee of a pension for life, social respect, and, in time, the highly respected title of privy councilor. Yet, to the dismay of his wife and friends, within three months Fontane resigned. The decision to turn his back on a secure and prestigious position with the Prussian government was clearly a painful one. Aside from his salary as a theater critic, which did not begin to cover annual expenses, he had no income beyond what he earned as a free-lance journalist. Correspondence makes it obvious, however, that he found his duties so unrewarding and the treatment he was accorded so demeaning that he was unable to hold out. In this period of intense duress he turned all the more passionately to the one consolation of his spirit, literature. The completion of the novel begun two decades earlier and postponed during the 1860s now became his primary goal.

The publication of *Vor dem Sturm* in 1878 signified the entrance of the novelist Fontane onto the German literary scene. It was hardly an auspicious beginning. The novel was viewed by some as too diffuse, by others as too long. Understandably, Fontane shelved plans for a novel of contemporary society, *Allerlei Glück* (All sorts of happiness), in favor of shorter works that were more likely to correspond to the reading tastes of the literary public and to assure him a quick financial return. By and large, his success in his first decade as a novelist remained modest. Not until the publication of *Irrungen, Wirrungen* (*Delusions, Confusions*) in 1887 did he really break into the front rank of contemporary writers of the Wilhelmine era.

The harvest of his last two decades is remarkable nevertheless. In the final 20 years of his life, the elderly writer continued almost uninterruptedly to turn out fiction while revising and expanding the relatively popular *Wanderungen,* along with ballads, occasional poetry, theater criticisms, and cultural commentaries. Two volumes of memoirs also appeared in his last decade. It was an unexpected burgeoning on the part of a hitherto journeyman writer and critic who, though he had held a respectable place in German letters, had never stood in its front ranks. Following the appearance in 1881 of *L'Adultera* (*The Woman Taken in Adultery*), he gradually hit his stride as a critic of contemporary life in his native land, becoming the skeptical chronicler of the age in all its achievements and excesses.

Advanced age gave Fontane's life a certain regularity. The legendary *old* Fontane, with piercing blue eyes, walrus mustache, and white hair now took the stage. Settled in on the upper floor of his apartment at 134c Potsdamer Straße, he could be seen almost daily strolling through the parks or along the canals and streets of Berlin. Summers were spent primarily in the Harz and Silesian Riesengebirge and, in his final years, at Karlsbad. In keeping with his habit of working on several projects at once, each in varying stages of development, almost every year saw the publication of one or more books. Until 1889 he remained theater critic of the *Vossische Zeitung,* at his post in Box 23 of the Royal Theater several times a week. Giving up the task at age 70, he nevertheless continued to report on the avant-garde presentations of the Freie Bühne, an organization dedicated to producing modern plays, which had opened in September 1889 with Ibsen's *Ghosts*. Although never completely won over to the tenets of naturalism, the old man remained a voice of critical support for the works of the younger generation throughout the last decade of his life. With characteristic skeptical objectivity, however, he tempered his enthusiasm by pointing out that despite novelty and artistic vitality, the unremitting pessimism and oftentimes mawkish sentimentality that infused many naturalist stage productions could scarcely long endure as the "intellectual daily bread of the nation" (HF III/2, 847).

Even though warmly acclaimed by proponents of the younger generation in German letters and awarded the Schiller Prize in 1891 and an honorary doctorate from the Friedrich-Wilhelm-Universität in Berlin in 1894, the overall lack of recognition from official circles, and especially from the aristocracy, wounded the aged writer. The absence of nobility among the guests at the public celebration of his seventieth birthday rankled deeply. "Modern Berlin has made an idol of me, but old Prussia, which I have glorified for more than forty years, . . . this 'old Prussia' has scarcely done a thing," he commented bitterly.[15] The irony that precisely that segment of society that he had most sharply criticized, the bourgeoisie, including the Jewish intellectual class, now offered him homage did not escape him.

Fontane's last years were also marked by an increasing skepticism concerning the empire. Added to his criticism of the rampant decline of cultural values in the Reich was his repudiation of its increasing militarism and jingoism and of what he took to be the increasingly byzantine nature of Wilhelm II's ostentatious reign. Although expressing himself in his fiction with a gentler touch, his letters both to the district judge Georg Friedlaender and to his friend from England James Morris testify eloquently to his growing disillusionment with the moribund aristocracy and the bourgeoisie, as well as to his recognition that the future of Europe lay with the lower classes, which in intelligence, industry, and potential he felt no longer needed to defer to the old social order.

Despite a severe physical and psychic illness that caused Fontane for a time to abandon work on the novel *Effi Briest* in 1892, his literary output scarcely diminished even with the increasing infirmities of his late seventies. On his physician's advice he turned for a time to writing his memoirs as a form of therapy and was able to regain a significant measure of productivity. Almost miraculously, the production of fictional works, reviews, commentaries, poems, revisions, and letters—he was one of the great correspondents of the German language—continued almost unabated. At his death on 20 September 1898, next to a list for review copies of his last novel, *Der Stechlin,* a brief poem entitled "Als ich zwei dicke Bände herausgab" ("On Publishing Two Thick Volumes"), ironically celebrating the concurrent appearance of both the novel and his second volume of memoirs at such an advanced age, lay on his desk.

Chapter Two
Antiquarianism and Romantic Destiny: *Vor dem Sturm*

Fontane was not a born storyteller, as his earliest novella, *Geschwisterliebe* (Sibling love, 1839), a hothouse romantic tale from his days as an apothecary's apprentice, proves. Stories written 15 years later for the journal *Argo* (1854), "James Monmouth" and "Tuch und Locke," although revealing a maturer hand, are also largely products of the conventional pseudohistorical literary baggage of the age and of the writer's romantic fascination with England. It is a truism of Fontane scholarship that his was a long and arduous path from the deeply embedded romantic literary conventions of his youth, which nourished much of his balladry, to the cool objectivity and social acumen characteristic of the great works of his old age. The dividing line between his early efforts and later mastery is marked by the journeyman decades of writing travel essays, beginning with *Ein Sommer in London* and culminating in the *Wanderungen durch die Mark Brandenburg*. That Fontane's essentially conventional literary education was balanced from the outset by a keen sense of contemporary engagement and social awareness is evidenced by his early political writings and translations of certain English poets of the industrial revolution. Nevertheless, the development of objectivity and a careful sense of observation of both persons and places, honed on his excursions through the rural byways of Brandenburg as well as at the editorial desk of the *Kreuzzeitung*, were necessary stages before the balladeer and journalist could evolve into the masterly social critic revered today. That the process extended well into his career as a writer of fiction is evidenced by the earliest products considered part of the canon of the mature Fontane.

The Novelist Emerges: *Vor dem Sturm*

The genesis of Fontane's first novel, *Vor dem Sturm* is complex. Correspondence with the north German writer Theodor Storm indicates that as early as 1854 Fontane had planned a fictional work devoted to the Prussian uprising against Napoleon in 1813. Nevertheless, the necessity of putting bread on the table time and again imposed postponement. His stays in England, years of work at the editorial desk of the *Kreuzzeitung,* weekly theater reviews, researching and writing the multiple volumes of *Wanderungen durch die Mark Brandenburg,* and the books devoted to the Prussian wars all kept him from carrying out his plan. Only after abortive starts in the 1860s and again in the first half of the 1870s was the project finally carried through in 1876–77. When at last serialized in the south German Catholic illustrated *Daheim* (At Home) in 1878, the novel had been over 20 years in the making. The book edition, contracted during the planning stage with Wilhelm Hertz, publisher of both the *Wanderungen* and the volumes on the Prussian wars, appeared in the autumn of 1878.

In four volumes encompassing 82 chapters, Fontane presents events in Prussia during the late winter of 1812 and spring of 1813, following the news of Napoleon's calamitous defeat during the Russian winter and "before the storm" of the Wars of Liberation. Primary figures are the Junker squire of Hohen-Vietz, Berndt von Vitzewitz, and his children, Lewin and Renate. Contrasted with them are their Berlin cousins, Tubal and Kathinka, son and daughter of the displaced Polish Count Ladalinski, who has taken service in Prussia after his homeland's political extinction. News of the French defeat inflames the elder Vitzewitz. Despite the reservations of many around him and the king's hesitation to break officially with their enforced allies, he presses an attack upon the demoralized French as they retreat through the Brandenburg countryside. His thirst for vengeance leads him to misconstrue local robberies as the acts of enemy marauders, and the plan to fall upon remnants of the Grande Armée with a troop of local militia culminates in a disastrous raid on the French garrison at Frankfurt an der Oder. In the battle, Lewin is captured, and Tubal is mortally wounded during an ensuing rescue mission. Interwoven with the political action is the story of the von Vitzewitz family, centering chiefly on Lewin's infatuation with Kathinka, who ultimately elopes with a rival, and Lewin's gradual recognition that true happiness is to be found with Marie Kniehase, an orphan girl who has grown up in the village.

Fontane's primary intent was to portray the spirit of the era by means of a broad panorama of episodes whose principal unifying element is the advent of anti-Napoleonic sentiment. In addition to influences of Scott and the earlier Prussian historical novelist Willibald Alexis, a basic structural principle, derived from Fontane's years as a balladeer and employed in later novels, is antithesis. Against the unpretentious and idyllic country life of Hohen-Vietz stands the eighteenth-century Francophile sophistication of Castle Guse, the estate of Berndt's sister, Amalie. Contrasting with the sense of unity with the land felt by the inhabitants of the manor house at Hohen-Vietz is the insecurity of the emigré Ladalinskis in Berlin. Villagers assembled in the inn at Hohen-Vietz have their parallels in the worthies who raise their steins in Berlin taverns; the Ladalinskis' ball is reflected in the parody of a petit bourgeois soirée in the rooms of Lewin's Berlin landlady, Frau Hulen, an episode anticipating the later novel *Frau Jenny Treibel* in its acerbic portrayal of the self-satisfied pettiness of the Berlin lower middle classes.

The same principle holds for the way the characters are treated. They too are generally cast as a series of opposites, without however, sinking into black and white: Lewin/Tubal, Renate-Marie/Kathinka, Seidentopf/Turgany, Dr. Faulstich/Hansen-Grell, Berndt von Vitzewitz/Privy Councilor Ladalinski. The antithetical principle works even in the overall structure of the books themselves, country atmosphere contrasting with the urban scene. Moreover, scenes in earlier sections prefigure later episodes. Thus the work's size notwithstanding, it was with some justice that the author could assert, "everything serves a purpose, everything is well thought out and is not simply there to fill out the pages" (HF I/3, 753).

Yet Fontane's satisfaction with the work's structure has not been shared. Despite felicities, *Vor dem Sturm* has the dubious distinction of being the writer's longest and most loosely constructed novel. There can be little doubt that the leisurely tempo and undemanding anecdotal style he had grown accustomed to after years of writing travelogues and battle descriptions led him to substantial errors of judgment in structure.

This was apparent from the outset. To his chagrin, even the editors of *Daheim* saw fit to shorten his work, cutting a quarter of its length. The complete book fared no better. Paul Heyse, Fontane's friend of two decades from the Tunnel and Germany's leading establishment writer, criticized its provincialism for a non-Prussian public and its verbose similarities to the *Wanderungen*. Fontane sought to meet such criticism by setting forth as his structural principle "the novel of multiplicity (*Vielheitsroman*), with all of its breadth and impediments, with its masses of portraiture and episodes,"[1] something that in more modern terms might be described as a technique of literary collage—more than a generation before Dos Passos and Döblin used it. Yet the realization of such an ambitious plan required greater discipline than the author of the leisurely *Wanderungen* was able to muster. The plot concerning the fortunes of the von Vitzewitz family, thin at best, is often nearly lost in the mass of detail and anecdote. Faint-hearted readers are likely to pale before lengthy and seemingly extraneous episodes inserted to present the general tenor of the age, or as adumbrative or retarding devices. With regard to the sections devoted to Kastalia, a literary group reminiscent of the Tunnel, for instance, one can only wish that in the literary discussions that make up long passages, Fontane had taken the advice of one of his characters concerning the ballad: "Imagination needs only to receive the correct stimulus; if this succeeds, one can boldly maintain, 'the less said, the better'" (HF I/3, 386).

Similarly, in another episode, a participant gives an eyewitness account of an engagement during the Spanish campaign, ending with a fallen officer whose coffin is placed before the altar of the cathedral. On one level, the historical perspective of the bloody reality of the Napoleonic wars is interjected into the otherwise relatively idyllic atmosphere of the novel. On another, the death of Tubal many chapters later and the laying out of his corpse before the altar of the village church is foreshadowed. Much the same applies to the description of the Battle of Borodino; it too offers historical background and prefigures the attack at Frankfurt an der Oder as well as far greater conflicts beyond the scope of the book and the price that will be paid for Prussia's freedom. Yet the length of these interludes, not to mention their similarity in form and function, seems out of proportion to their effect, no matter how subtle the authorial intent.

Even more problematic is the integration of an incongruous romanticism into a work purporting to be a realistic depiction of a crucial political epoch. Thus, interwoven with the historical action are the fortunes of the von Vitzewitz family, which have languished since an ancestor slew his brother many years before. A prophecy promises deliverance when after a purifying fire, "a princess enters the house" (HF I/3, 22). Fontane's dependence on such a device—the legacy of his years as a writer of ballads—indicates the extent to which he was still mired in the literary conventions of an earlier age. Its use also accounts for the diffusion of interest—the novel of multiplicity notwithstanding—associated with the lack of a clear-cut chief character. Berndt von

Vitzewitz, drawn in part from the person of Baron August Ludwig von der Marwitz, whose life Fontane had briefly recounted in Book III of the *Wanderungen,* personifies the desire for political renewal and liberation from the foreign yoke. Yet it is not he but his son Lewin, as the agent who fulfills the prophecy, who seems to be the chief figure. Lewin's liberation from the spell of Kathinka and discovery of his love for the orphan Marie through a process of clarifying dreams commands much of the foreground. Yet it is in essence a passive process, reflective of Fontane's Huguenot background in that it is ultimately seen as predestined.

Thus at the outset the Lewin-Marie action is presaged in the complex of motifs associated with a grave inscription "and [she] can walk on stars" (HF I/3, 12) discovered by Lewin in the first chapter. The star motif is soon associated with Marie, who as a child had danced in a dress with golden paper stars; as a tombstone inscription it connotes redemption—in Calvinistic terms, the privilege of the elect. Marie is thus almost from the beginning singled out to be the chosen instrument of fulfillment who will liberate the von Vitzewitz family from ill fortune, guarantee its succession, and provide for Lewin's happiness. Her singularity as one chosen by the incomprehensible grace of God is further ratified by the theological candidate Othegraven, who declares, "I have never seen Marie, except that with a kind of joyful certainty I have had the feeling: she will bring happiness and will be happy" (HF I/3, 120).

Events prove that Lewin too is among the elect. His revelatory dreams are invariably associated with or introduced by a view of the stars. Immediately before arriving at the village where he discovers the symbolic grave inscription comes the first suggestion that his life is governed by a benign destiny: "The stars shone forth ever more numerous. Lewin lifted his cap to let the fresh winter air pass over his brow and looked up with astonishment and reverence at the sparkling heavens. It seemed to him as if all the dark fortunes, the legacy of his house, fell away from him and as if brightness and radiance from above poured into his soul" (HF I/3, 10).

Although seemingly a conservative work, in which Fontane sought "glorification of love of fatherland going beyond mere more or less affected 'loyalty,' "[2] *Vor dem Sturm* was by no means intended as chauvinistic propaganda. "It stands for religion, morality, and fatherland," argued the author, "but it is full of hate for the blue cornflower [a traditional Hohenzollern symbol] and 'With God for King and

Fatherland.'"[3] Thus even though richly nourished by traditional Prussian values, Fontane saw it as a document directed against the militaristic jingoism of the Second Reich. Indeed, in the outcome of the Lewin-Marie action the book is deeply infused with a liberal ideology that points to a Prussia revitalized not only by its aristocracy but by its lower classes. At stake is not just Berndt's and Lewin's part in the historical events of the epoch but the renewal of the von Vitzewitz clan itself. The chosen individual proves to be an orphan of dubious lineage, whose primary qualities the reader must take on faith, since little actually demonstrates Marie's inner nobility. Her destiny together with the heroism of Othegraven and the poet Hansen-Grell make clear, however, that it is neither birth nor lineage but character which is the stuff of true nobility. Fontane employs the cynical, hence all the more credible, General Bamme to make his point regarding the chief message spread by the French: "Not much will come of that brotherhood of theirs nor of that freedom business either. But as for what they've put in the middle, they've got something there. After all, when you get right down to it, what else does it amount to except: a human being is a human being" (HF I/3, 706).

The ethical-political implications of *Vor dem Sturm* are also significant. Questions concerning the justification of undeclared guerrilla war, the primacy of the social over the political order, the nature of the Prussian character as viewed from outside, and, most significant, the legitimacy of individual action for the sake of country counter to the will of legitimate authority, were by no means academic in Germany, especially in the years between 1933 and 1945. That Fontane did not resolve them unambiguously is attested by the fact that *Vor dem Sturm* was reissued in 1944.

Yet, despite its sometimes tedious and seemingly meandering structure, *Vor dem Sturm* must be reckoned a remarkable achievement. If it is possible to speak of apprenticeship in the work of a 60-year-old professional with decades of experience behind him, the term can be applied here. Many of the qualities that distinguish later works by Fontane, including expansive techniques of foreshadowing[4] and scintillating dialogue, are present here. Moreover, its historical patina notwithstanding, in its dinner parties, excursions, and conversational exchanges *Vor dem Sturm* reveals a strong tendency toward the traditional novel of upper-class society that became the writer's forte.

To be sure, compared with the greatest historical novel of the Napoleonic era, Tolstoy's *War and Peace*, written a decade earlier, *Vor dem*

Sturm lacks sweep and focus. Indeed, such a comparison strikingly underscores the provincialism, even backwardness, of the German novel in the first years of the Second Empire. It is in fact a measure of the paucity of excellent historical novels in German (only Stifter's highly stylized *Witiko* is a serious contender, and that is Austrian in its background) that Peter Demetz's judgment of it as the finest German historical novel[5] is entirely valid.

Chapter Three
Balladry and Psychology: Finding the Way

The lateness of his decision at age 56 to devote himself to fiction after years of balladry and journalistic prose did not mean that the evolution of Fontane's fictional talent was by any means complete. He had yet to find the way. In *Vor dem Sturm,* both a moribund romanticism as well as the leisurely anecdotal tempo and tendency to extraneous detail characteristic of the *Wanderungen* still guided his pen. Not surprisingly, *Grete Minde* and *Ellernklipp* (Alder cliff), more compact tales of vengeance, murder, and fate, which came on the heels of the novel, were also quickly recognized as vestiges of his earlier development and characterized by contemporary critics as "balladesque."[1] Indeed, both may be seen as prose versions of the *Moritat,* the German folk ballad dealing with gruesome and sensational events.

Certainly Fontane cannot be faulted for the gradualness of his literary development, yet it is clear that the superabundance of ballad-like tendencies, the legacy of the Tunnel, and a manifestation of the obsession of German culture in the nineteenth century with antiquarianism relegated these stories to an outmoded aesthetic even when they were new. That they were generally well received at the time is, of course, an indication not only of how well they are crafted, but, even more, of how much they fit the pseudohistoricism characteristic of their gilded age.

Modern literary criticism, influenced by the author's later achievements and unsympathetic to the antiquarianism of the era, tends to dismiss them. Regardless of how their antiquarianism is viewed, however, they stand as significant transitional works. Above all, the desire to meet the demands of periodicals for short fiction provided a school of discipline in which Fontane learned to curb the tendency to expansiveness that mars *Vor dem Sturm*. Furthermore, the misbegotten concept of the novel of multiplicity, not really compatible with Fontane's genius, and the inclination to portray in breadth were abandoned for a concentration in depth.

Grete Minde: The Psychological Task

With this relatively long novella, written in the latter half of 1878 and early 1879, Fontane sought to keep his name before the public while awaiting reaction to *Vor dem Sturm.* To the editor of a popular journal he reported on 3 April 1879 (HF IV/3, 19) that he was currently sketching a novel of contemporary Berlin life provisionally entitled *Allerlei Glück* (All sorts of happiness). Thus already at this stage Fontane felt that historical fiction was not the only area in which he was inclined to try his hand. Yet the uncertainty of another extended project led him to abandon the undertaking for the briefer form of the novella. Not only was the latter held in higher regard than the novel in German critical circles but, easier to publish, it also guaranteed a speedier financial return. Obviously that was something very much on the author's mind since the new story was the first he undertook as an independent writer. Thus, even before beginning, he was careful to negotiate length and content with the editors of the magazine *Nord und Süd,* as well as to contract for a book edition with his usual publisher, Wilhelm Hertz.

The subject of *Grete Minde* was again drawn from the ethos of the *Wanderungen* and the chronicles of Mark Brandenburg. Tangermünde, a small town in the Altmark, west of Berlin, had been severely damaged by fire in 1617. Margarete Minde, the daughter of a ne'er-do-well from one of the town's patrician families, denied her patrimony by her uncle, a town councilor, had been held responsible. In the company of her husband and a vagrant, she was burned at the stake in 1619. So much for the historical facts. An ongoing legacy of the *Wanderungen* and *Vor dem Sturm* was the desire to portray "a picture of the customs and character types from the period following the Thirty Years War."[2]

Fontane characterized the material as "a brilliant historical topic" (HF I/1, 878). Beyond its antiquarian content, however, undoubtedly as a result of his studies for the aborted contemporary novel, a new creative impulse emerged in *Grete Minde:* the desire to display to the world "that when the material suggests it, I can also solve 'a psychological problem' and tell a story without retarding passages."[3] Thus psychological causality, the depiction of how "Grete Minde, child of a patrician family, provoked by greed, prejudice, and unwillingness to compromise on her family's part and even more as a result of the defiance in her own heart, comes to her end in more or less grand fashion, destroying herself and half the town,"[4] now became the goal.

As he had in preparing the *Wanderungen,* Fontane undertook substantial research on the background of the events he depicted, including visits to the area. Local chronicles provided him with names (Emerenz, Zernitz, Peter Guntz, etc.) and salient incidents, including the explosion during the puppet play—which in fact occurred almost three decades after the time of the story. Significantly, the era of the Thirty Years War was abandoned in favor of the period of religious uncertainty following the Reformation. Through this alteration, a principal idea, the collision between the love and solicitude sought by Grete and faith without good works, upheld by the representatives of orthodox Lutheranism, is extended beyond the personalities of the novella and embedded in the age itself.

Familiarity with later works by Fontane make it difficult to evaluate *Grete Minde* objectively. His essentially modern desire to master the psychological problem seems at odds with the archaic tendencies with which he embellished the story. He was, for instance, particularly proud of his skill at rendering archaic speech. Given the antiquarian tendencies of the age, not to mention his own literary development, it is no surprise that he should seek to wrap his nineteenth-century case study in pseudohistorical drapery. Nevertheless the almost patronizing quaintness of the chronicle tone cannot help but strike the modern reader as alien and poorly integrated with the psychological aspects of the story.[5] Fortunately, abandonment of antiquarian topics soon rendered the problem moot; Fontane's sensitivity to nuances of speech was turned to more fruitful use in the masterful contemporary dialogue of the works to follow.

Fontane's story describes events in the life of the title character from adolescence to her self-immolation less than a decade later as an avenging angel. The child of her father's second marriage to a Spanish Catholic, Grete is considered an outsider, especially by her stepbrother Gerd and his prudish wife, Trud. The hostility to which Grete is subjected after her father's death impels her to flee with her young neighbor Valtin before she reaches her majority. Several years after they have found asylum with a wandering troupe of puppet players (a motif Fontane borrowed from Storm's *Pole Poppenspäler*), Valtin dies, begging Grete to return and make peace with her family. Notwithstanding her smoldering resentment, she nevertheless fulfills her promise for the sake of their child. Her brother, however, rejects Grete and her child and is supported by the town council in his denial of her patrimony. Driven to madness by injustice and hatred, Grete sets fire to the town and dies in the conflagration.

Even though her ethnic and religious background set Grete apart from the beginning, she is not intrinsically an outsider. Her legitimate place in the Minde family is undermined primarily by her sister-in-law, the prudish, malicious, and embittered Trud, who envies the girl's captivating nature and works to diminish her place in the family hierarchy. Grete's absolute need for familial security is based on the insecurity she feels about her origins. She must prove that she is a member of the socioreligious community, and does so even for the strict pastor Gigas. So long as her father is alive she is secure in her brother's house, but after his death Trud's envy and hostility set the tone. In fact, as Valtin assures her, Grete is loved by others, but the only affection she seeks is bound up with her sense of identity; she wishes to be loved not as an individual, but through the love of Trud and Gerd to have her rightful place in the family acknowledged. In the last analysis, Grete Minde seeks confirmation of her selfhood, a quest encapsulated for her in the biblical admonition of her dying father to Trud: "Let the orphans find mercy with thee" (HF I/1, 37).

Denied this confirmation by the loveless atmosphere of her brother's house, Grete attempts to find a surrogate in the outside world. In stories and fairy tales she discovers justification for leaving her home. As is almost always the case in Fontane's oeuvre, orthodox religion fails in a moment of crisis. Preoccupied with his sermon to the Electoral Prince, Gigas provides only ambiguities when Grete turns to him for advice; these she interprets as a license to flee. Valtin, however, ultimately compels her to admit her real reason, which is her inability "either to see injustice or to suffer any" (HF I/1, 57).

The similarity of Fontane's novella to Kleist's *Michael Kohlhaas* has frequently been pointed out. There is, however, a significant difference between these two works by Prussian masters: Kleist's figure seeks the return of physical property; his is a quest for acknowledgment of an inherently just state and, by inference, a just world. Grete Minde's demand is more personal and limited. She seeks acknowledgment of the legitimacy of her person; her first goal is self-justification and only at the end does she seek legal amends for what has been denied to her on a personal level.

Walter Müller-Seidel has pointed out the work's nature as a negative fairy tale, one that ends not with "happily ever after" but with its opposite.[6] In essence, this is an extension of Grete Minde's existential problem. Neither in her brother's house nor in the world outside is she able to find the acknowledgment for which she yearns. The fairy-tale world on which she bases her flight is exposed as a delusion. No miraculous intervention, such as the stag that in answer to a lost maiden's prayers to the Virgin carried her to safety on its antlers, appears for Grete. The realm envisioned by Valtin, where there is "no war and no sickness, and the people who live there love one another, grow old and die without pain" (HF I/1, 32), also proves elusive, and the sense of belonging Grete had desired at home does not emerge in the outside world either. A favorite Fontane motif, a drifting raft, suggesting Grete's loosened ties with the entire social order, underscores the hopelessness of her situation. Its ramshackle structure proves the closest thing to the antlers of the miraculous stag she and her companion ever encounter. Moreover, the suspicious appearance of their companions prompts them to seek flight even while fleeing.

Fontane compresses the intervening years of their exile; yet it is obvious that one disillusionment has followed upon another. Valtin, whom Grete had singled out as her knight, has been a hapless and ineffectual champion. His life and death are pathetically unheroic. In Grete's affiliation with itinerant puppet players, Fontane combines her complete loss of ties to her identity in the patrician social order with the motif of the Last Judgment and final retribution with which the work concludes.

Grete's guilt, the author is at pains to make clear, has grown from love denied and from her defiant unwillingness to accept the injustice meted out to her. Not only the inscription from the wall of the town hall, which Grete cites after the rejection of her suit by the town council, but especially the marionette play of the Last Judgment, interwoven throughout the story, endow her final act with eschatological significance. In the final holocaust she becomes not the angel of heavenly fulfillment but an agent of divine retribution against her stepbrother and sister-in-law and the entire social order because of their failure to carry out the biblical injunction with which her dying father had entrusted her to her family.

The history of the work's reception is a classic example of the relativity of taste. On its appearance, *Grete Minde* was greeted with some acclaim, and only a few years later was included in Paul Heyse's *Deutscher Novellenschatz* (*Treasury of German Novellas*). Not surprisingly, more recent critics have been less impressed. Conrad Wandrey, whose early scholarly study set attitudes that have never ceased to be influential, found *Grete Minde* inherently anachronistic,[7] while Peter Demetz (Demetz, 97) maintained that the work's interweaving of determinism and history reflects "an instinctive pupil of Taine in a gown borrowed from Dürer," revealing "the unhappy plight of an age without style." Müller-Seidel (Müller-Seidel, 88) also argues that the historical trappings and archaic language are superficial, essentially vestiges of Fontane's ballad style, which contribute nothing essential to the meaning of the story.

Although nothing in Fontane's letters and comments appears to support such views, Marxist critics have attempted to interpret the work as a veiled appeal to the ruling classes of the Second Reich for social justice.[8] It has been pointed out, however, that although Fontane was certainly not unaware of inequities in the Reich, there is little in *Grete Minde* to justify such an interpretation. The heroine is not really inferior to those who treat her unjustly, and if she becomes so, it is by her own volition. Moreover, her destruction of the city does not bring about a more equitable social order. Finally, had this been even the secondary intent of the work, it would seem to have been an utter failure. Nowhere in contemporary reviews do we find evidence that Fontane's story was understood as an appeal for social justice.

Despite stylistic weaknesses, *Grete Minde* is not without its graces. Except for a cloying beginning—children were never Fontane's strong point—in its juxtaposition of events the story has been compared to a woodcut whose garish colors sharply contrast with one another.[9] The basic techniques of Fontane's craft throughout his career as a novelist, such as the revelation of character through dialogue, scenic prefigurations, and rich symbolic connotations, although somewhat heavy-handedly used, are much in evidence here. The final conflagration is prefigured not only by Grete's vision at her father's grave and by the puppet play of the Last Judgment but by the explosion of fireworks with which the play ends. Grete's need for love is symbolized by the linnet's nest with which the tale begins, and the outcome of the entire story is foreshadowed in the fairy tale of the juniper tree, according to which an unloved stepchild, mistreated and finally murdered by the wicked stepmother, turns into a bird and avenges itself by killing her with fire and flame. In an extension of this, the desire for free and open spaces is frequently associated with the chief figure, and birdlike qualities are attributed to her.[10]

Above all, however, it is the psychological concentration that represents the most significant achievement in *Grete Minde*. Obviously, psychological verisimilitude played a role in the characteristics of *Vor dem Sturm*, but it had not yet assumed a central interest except in the larger sense of showing how "the great feeling born at that time found its way to the most varied individuals and the effect it had upon them."[11] In *Grete Minde,* however, Fontane from the outset set about delineating a character who could credibly be responsible for the calamity with which the work concludes. At the same time, he also undertook to establish an environment and sequence of events that make the ultimate catastrophe, if not inevitable, at least comprehensible. Thus as Demetz (Demetz, 94ff) has pointed out, *Grete Minde* may be viewed as a case of psychological determinism. Yet, as we shall see, such a psychological approach is the underlying principle of many of Fontane's novels, including most of those in which social content commands the foreground. The pattern of *Grete Minde,* the creation of a believable character in a sequence of events that makes her act comprehensible, is, simply put, the chief trait of Theodor Fontane's realism. In later works, in the place of an extraordinary criminal offense, it is social transgressions and violations of the accepted moral code that are portrayed. Fontane's development towards such a principle, his further refinements of it, and its consequences for his art—primarily the abandonment of the literary antiquarianism in which he had been mired—is in essence the chronicle of his evolution to his place in German letters.

Ellernklipp: Vestigial Romanticism

Through his niece Anna von Below, Fontane found the material for *Ellernklipp* (Alder cliff) while vacationing in the Harz Mountains in August of 1878. The local tale of the murder of a young hunter by his jealous father, after he had been discovered with a foster sister, provided the basic story. Tradition held that the father hid himself on a cliff overlooking the town, and overcome by remorse on hearing his son's funeral bells, threw himself to his death. Church records confirmed part of the story and suggested the subtitle (after a church chronicle from the Harz Mountains). The landscape around Ilsenburg and Wernigerode, renamed Emmerode in the novella, yielded local color.

Although, in a letter of 19 November 1878 (HF I/3, 894), Fontane indicated that he had already sketched the general outlines of the work, it was not until the following September that he began writing it. By the end of November 1879 he had completed a first draft, and along with the recently sketched *Schach von Wuthenow*, offered it to the editor of the prestigious *Westermanns Monatshefte* on 14 March 1880. The choice fell on *Ellernklipp* and the author set to work in earnest. Although Fontane's duties as a theater critic, his work on other projects, and his own meticulous revisions delayed the undertaking, *Ellernklipp* appeared in *Westermanns Monatshefte* without chapter titles in May and June of 1881. A book edition, chapter titles restored, followed later the same year.

As in *Grete Minde,* the psychological element dominates in *Ellernklipp*. Grete evolves from an innocent child into a murderess. A similar challenge was offered by the development of Baltzer Bocholtz from an upright and responsible pillar of the community to a man who in a fit of passion kills his son. Although we are not given an entire life's story, the psychological inevitability suggested by the character's grim earnestness and sternness, the fear he inspires in others, as well as Baltzer's inner monologue before his crime all work to make its likelihood convincing. Yet the causal chain of unalterable psychological determinism is not the final principle at work here. Once more the author drew on romantic literary convention, which, in the form of a fateful higher power, has the final word.

Fontane's alterations of his source material make evident his intention of fashioning something more traditionally poetic than a story of jealousy, murder, and suicide. Although the alder trees of the title suggest mysterious forces in the German cultural tradition, it is not the name of the cliff, but the cliff itself as a place of destiny that is significant. Thus, as the title makes clear, *Ellernklipp* is a *Schicksalsnovelle,* a novella of fate. The cliff, traditionally only the site of the father's atonement, now becomes associated also with the original crime so that it is both the locale of murder and the site of retribution. One cannot help but be reminded of the motto inscribed on the *Judenbuche* (Jew's beech tree) in Annette von Droste-Hülshoff's famous tale of the same name. In that, as in *Ellernklipp,* the inevitability of retribution is suggested by the guilty man's inherent fear of the site of his crime, just as the portentous saying of the clairvoyant Melcher Harms, "eternal and inalterable is the law" (HF I/1, 153), implies that the same covenant of an eye for an eye holds in both works. Retribution as part of the mysterious workings of nature is also evident in the function assigned to the moon, which appears as "a blood red disc, large and questioning" (HF I/1, 176), at the time of the murder and at salient points thereafter, and ultimately provoking the murderer's self-imposed punishment.[12]

By the time of *Ellernklipp* the *Schicksalsnovelle* had long been a conventional favorite of nineteenth-century German writers. Indeed, fateful forces, cursed locations, objects, and dates had already become a literary commonplace by the late eighteenth century. By the onset of the next they commanded both the stage in the infamous *Schicksalstragödie* (fate tragedy) in such works as Werner's *Der 24. Februar,* parodied by Platen in *Die verhängnisvolle Gabel* (The fateful fork), and the narrative in works such as Brentano's *Die Geschichte vom braven Kasperl und dem schönen Annerl* (The tale of upright Kasper and fair Annie) (1817). It is not difficult to see in them a variant of the traditional form long dearest to Fontane's heart, the ballad. Indeed, as Walter Müller-Seidel (Müller-Seidel, 82) points out, categories of crime and punishment, guilt and atonement, as well as of poetic justice, remained vital literary constituents in German literature throughout the nineteenth century. By 1880, however, they had become a tired convention, a point that no doubt had something to do with the more reserved reception accorded *Ellernklipp* than had been accorded *Grete Minde*.

Other problems as well weaken the work. As with *Vor dem Sturm*, a diffusion of interest between two characters undermines its effectiveness. Describing the story, Fontane singled out not the murderer but Hilde, Baltzer's foster child, as the main character (HF IV/3, 66). Yet she remains more of an idea than a person, more literary creation than flesh and blood. In her the author admitted he had attempted to depict "the daemonic-irresistible power of illegitimacy and the languid personality" (HF IV/3, 66). Yet despite Fontane's attempt to flesh out Hilde's person, by virtue of her passivity, languidity, and general morbidity, in short by virtue of her literary origins, she is scarcely a convincing figure and remains more romantic *belle dame* than orphaned waif from the Harz mountains.

Almost everything, from the title and the fatalistic trappings of the work to the murder itself, tends to thrust the far stronger figure of Bocholtz into the foreground. For this reason the final chapters, in which Hilde at last establishes a loving relationship with her hitherto estranged grandmother, seem almost an appendage. Like Ottilie in Goethe's *Die Wahlverwandschaften* (*Elective Affinities*) with whom she is frequently compared, she becomes almost saintly. Nevertheless, there is more literature than life on these pages. Similarly, the figures of the countess's guests, whose sole function it is to introduce the concept of *languissance,* an idea far beyond the sensibilities of the primitive mountain folk who otherwise people the tale, is a clumsy intrusion and adds nothing but an unnecessary literary flourish.

Breakthrough: *Schach von Wuthenow* and the Prussian Soul

Like its predecessors, *Schach von Wuthenow* (translated as *A Man of Honor*) is the fictional treatment of an actual event. Unlike the others, however, the work was consciously endowed by the author with a significance transcending the event itself. In the autumn of 1815, as a means of resolving his heavy indebtedness, Major Otto Ludwig Friedrich von Schack, of the elite Prussian cavalry Regiment Gensdarmes, already in his fifties, offered to marry a well-to-do but unattractive woman of the Huguenot colony in Berlin. Shortly before the engagement was to be made public, however, fearing the ridicule of his comrades for what would be perceived as a desperate move, von Schack did away with himself.

Gossip and fantasy sensationalized this tragicomedy over the years. The graying von Schack became a handsome young lieutenant involved in a bit of high-spirited fun, and the victimized woman, in reality well over 30, was transformed into a young girl who was expecting his child. In an added piquancy, her mother was made to appeal to the king, who commanded his officer to restore the daughter's honor by marriage. This was the tale Fontane had from a family friend, Mathilde von Rohr (1810–1889), some 20 years before beginning the novella. He even seems to have met and corresponded with the 75-year-old Fräulein von Crayen, the original of his fictional heroine.

Fontane's interest in the Schack material was apparently renewed by work on *Vor dem Sturm* and by May 1878 it was one of a number of topics under consideration as possible subjects for stories following the publication of his first novel. At this time too, the author began to envision Major von Schack's end as symptomatic of Prussian demoralization before the Battle of Jena (14 October 1806), in which the army, having "fallen asleep on the laurels of Frederick the Great," as Queen Luise had put it, suffered a devastating defeat at the hands of Napoleon. Although *Schach von Wuthenow* was apparently first drafted in 1879, progress was slow, extending over a period of almost three years and involving substantial research.[13] It was not until mid-August

1882, after the appearance of the first half in the *Vossische Zeitung,* that Fontane was finally able to report to his wife that he had put the final touches on the work. The book, revised anew, was published late in 1882 (with the imprint 1883) by the house of Wilhelm Friedrich in Leipzig.

Fontane's version is a substantial elaboration of what he had learned from Mathilde von Rohr. In the Berlin of 1805 and the first half of 1806, the salon of the beautiful widow von Carayon and her pockmarked daughter Victoire is frequented by officers of the prestigious Regiment Gensdarmes. The most attractive is Squadron Captain (*Rittmeister*) von Schach, who is rumored to have a relationship with the mother. Regaled one evening by Prince Louis Ferdinand on the hidden beauty of the ugly, the impressionable Schach finds Victoire alone a few nights later and both succumb to the passion of the instant. Relying on Schach's honor, Victoire avoids revealing what has transpired until several months later. Then, in revulsion brought on by an unrelated prank organized by Schach's regiment, she confesses her situation to her mother. Confronted, Schach agrees to marriage, then disappears. Embarrassed by caricatures ridiculing his apparent inability to choose between mother and daughter, he has withdrawn to his ancestral manor to sort things out. Misunderstanding his silence, Frau von Carayon entreats the king to intercede. Called to account, Schach goes through with the wedding but shoots himself almost immediately afterwards. Letters form an epilogue. In the first, Bülow, an outspoken critic of the Prussian scene, describes what has happened as a symptom of the decline of values and the worship of a false sense of honor that has led Prussia to ruin. From a personal perspective, Victoire's letter that follows reflects on the inner reasons for her husband's death.

Again it was the psychological factor that attracted the author. At the same time, because Schach is representative of the spirit of his age, Fontane's psychological analysis of him is applicable not only to his individual case but in part to the entire society he represents. Thus with *Schach von Wuthenow* Fontane undertook the first of his probing critiques of the Prussian character. Various sections, especially early chapters, tell us as much about the aristocratic-militaristic society of Berlin—and not only in the first decade of the nineteenth century—as they do about Schach. It is obvious that the Prussian royal residence is an armed camp. Parades pass the von Carayon balcony almost daily, a full-dress revue is one of the highlights of the summer season, and the von Carayon ladies consider themselves fortunate to count officers of the celebrated Regiment Gensdarmes as regular guests. For the latter, however, although the successes of Bonaparte have made it evident that Prussia's future is by no means secure, horses, hobbies, socializing, gossip, and tasteless pranks constitute their vacuous pastimes and suggest their ripeness for a fall.

On another level too, *Schach von Wuthenow* also represents a significant advance. Although still a historical subject, and in atmosphere close to *Vor dem Sturm,* the proximity to the novels of contemporary Berlin society is evident. The process begun in the first novel to produce "something stimulating, cheerful, if possible refined and intelligent conversation, as is customary in this country,"[14] unfolds in the drawing-room exchanges of this novella. Character is revealed not only through the hints of a sophisticated and somewhat ironic narrator but by means of adroit touches of gesture and speech. Typical Fontane episodes and locations predominate—the salon, the excursion, the dinner party. Typically too, it is not only what individuals say but also—taking into consideration the standpoint of the speaker—what is said about them by others that enables the reader to build a full picture of the personalities in the story.

Fontane is at pains to enable the reader to understand Schach even before the character begins to develop. In the opinion of his brother officers, he posesses "a very peculiar personality, which, regardless of whatever other things one might find in it, presents at the very least some psychological problems" (HF I/1, 571). Apart from his high standards regarding integrity and marriage, he is described as pathologically sensitive to the opinions of others, especially to those of his peers. The possibility that Schach will marry the widow von Carayon is rejected by a comrade, simply because he knows Schach could not deal with the necessity of introducing her disfigured daughter as his stepdaughter. Yet in many respects Schach is seen to represent the paradoxical finest and worst aspects of Prussian character. For all his caste-centered rigidity he is, we are told, at the same time a man of complete integrity, honesty, and chivalry, "one of our best, . . . and *really* a good man" (HF I/1, 572).

That someone with such political and moral limitations should be considered a paragon of the Prussian officer class presages little good for Prussia in the opinion of Bülow, the character Fontane introduces for objective commentary. He dismisses Schach as the personification of the "Prussian narrowness" that unfailingly believes in the absolute security of the Prussian state by virtue of the Prussian army, the irresistible power of the Prussian infantry attack, and finally, that no battle is lost as long as the Regiment Gensdarmes has not yet attacked (HF I/1 393), a judgment ironically confirmed a few pages later when Schach repeats the first principle in conversation with Frau von Carayon.

Like Count Bninski in *Vor dem Sturm,* with whom he also shares an objectivity acquired beyond Prussian borders, Bülow evaluates the world by a measure other than the Prussian officer's riding whip. A provocative conversationalist and dissenter, he misses no chance to criticize Prussia's politics, its cultural values, and mindless militarism. Much of what he says is, of course, intended merely to be outrageous, and a good deal of it, as historically astute readers know, also proves to be inaccurate. In this respect, he is a typically ambiguous character of the sort found throughout Fontane's oeuvre. As an additional touch of irony, the skeptic is endowed with a trait of sentimentality that functions to further undermine confidence in his opinions. His significance extends, however, far beyond his immediate role. With him the skeptical ambiguity characteristic of Fontane, initially suggested by General Bamme in *Vor dem Sturm,* comes to the fore. Readers of 1882, little more than a decade after the founding of the Second Reich, could hardly overlook Bülow's comments on the historical role of Prussia, its army and its official state religion, especially in an era when the empire was at loggerheads with Rome while still preening itself on its military accomplishments.

Fontane's interweaving of the political with the private, the fate of Prussia and Schach's own destiny, reveals his art at a new level of mastery. Events leading to Victoire's seduction provide an example. After a discussion in which von Bülow repeats his reservations regarding the hollow spirit of the Prussian army, Prince Louis Ferdinand holds forth on Victoire and the relativity of beauty. Although forewarned by Bülow regarding the unreliability of royalty in such matters, the prince's remarks do not fail to make an impression on Schach, who recalls them at the crucial moment with Victoire. As a bridge, Fontane inserts a pair of events having reference to both aspects of the story. Against a glowing sunset, a flotilla of swans silently passes in review on the river before the prince's palace. The same motif is taken up in the next chapter in what is called by a prophetic relative of Schach's "the farewell review of the Frederickian army" (HF I/1, 612). The enigma of beauty and splendor in their varied guises is inherent in both episodes, as is the unmistakable association of a swan song with the transistoriness of both.

The high point of Fontane's interweaving of the private and the political, and another example of his combining seemingly unconnected anecdotal material with telling symbolic effect, is the episode devoted to the parody by members of Schach's regiment of Zacharias Werner's Martin Luther drama, *Die Weihe der Kraft* (The dedication of strength). The Regiment Gensdarmes was known for such high jinks, and the summer sleigh ride did in fact transpire. Within the story, of course, the bawdy transvestite burlesque of Luther and his relationship to Katharina von Bora reflects Bülow's diagnosis of the decadence of the Prussian spirit. In their caricature of the great reformer, in the view of Schach, Alvensleben, and Bülow a personage decidedly not for mockery, the junior officers of Regiment Gensdarmes betray the shallowness of their commitment to the historical and religious tradition of Prussia, already characterized by Bülow as bound to Luther's church. At the same time, the ribald travesty reminds Victoire of her own illicit relationship with the self-proclaimed monk, Schach. Overcome with self-revulsion, she douses herself with cologne and purges herself by confessing to her mother. It is a final irony that Schach, who shares a repugnance for such tastelessness, has not been among the participants in the event that leads to his undoing.

The newly evolved amplitude of Fontane's symbolic art reaches yet another high point in Schach's visit to Schloß Wuthenow,[15] to which he retires after malicious caricatures have forced him to leave Berlin. The episode is a paradigm of symbolic recapitulation. The imagery of Schach's run-down ancestral home with its inner decay, and moths caught behind the window panes, his aimless wandering through the pergola flanking the park, and circular path around an oak tree, which, as Demetz (Demetz, 161) suggests, Fontane in fact spoils by making too obvious, all suggest Schach's quandary and its outcome. The same applies to his sleep as his boat drifts out on a dead arm of the lake. His discovery of two scenes from the life of Frederick the Great surrounded by wreaths of everlasting—a favorite of Fontane's in suggesting death and recollection—with ribbons of Prussian colors, signals the outlook not only for Schach but for Frederick's Prussia as well. Even Schach's decision not to discuss his plight with Pastor Bienengräber, his recognition that, although knowing the commandments, he lacks the desire to obey them, underscores the laxity of his commitment to the precepts of the Lutheran church and the principles on which the Frederickian state has been built. In similar fashion, family portraits place him against a tradition of duty unto death, suggesting the almost comic aspect of his inability to come to terms with what life demands of him and the hopelessness of his situation as he views it.

Yet a sense of enigma remains. Fontane presents the reader with a relatively detailed analysis of Schach's personality as seen through his closest comrades and creates a tightly meshed chain of events leading to the final step. His relationship to the mother rather than the daughter, his commitment to an unmarried existence, his numbing sense of image and dread of withdrawal from the vortex of life in the royal capital to the boredom of his estate, above all the embarrassment this vainly handsome officer feels when compelled to marry a disfigured woman, who in his better moments he pities but does not love, all add up to a wealth of motivation; yet do they justify suicide? In concluding the novella with two letters that bring home the dual nature of the study, as political criticism on the one hand and as a psychological case study on the other, Fontane attempts to allay such questions, albeit not with complete success.

There is critical disagreement concerning the validity of the final letters. Interpreters who view the novella primarily as a cultural-political document argue that Bülow's letter reflects the author's essential point of view. Peter Demetz (Demetz, 163), however, argues convincingly that by placing Victoire's letter at the very end, Fontane would seem to be subordinating the political statement to the private point of view.

Bülow's letter is a minor treatise on the flaws of Prussian militarism. Dated only weeks before the catastrophe of Jena and Auerstedt—history vindicates the opinion of an otherwise fallible character—it brings home the analogy Fontane wishes to be made between Schach and the uniquely Prussian aspect of his case, "which could have occurred in this manner and form only in His Royal Prussian Majesty's residence and capital city or, if outside the latter, only in the ranks of our post-Frederickian army" (HF I/1, 678). The Prussian army immediately before its most inglorious defeat, in which incidentally the Regiment Gensdarmes, held in reserve during the battle, was compelled to capitulate during the retreat and was subsequently disbanded (Sagave, 120), is dismissed as an army in which arrogant caste conceit has displaced a true ideal of honor, and in which genuine morale and esprit de corps have succumbed to a spirit of unthinking mechanical obedience. Such an army has been no match for the inspired leadership of Napoleon, which has been extolled several times in the course of the story. The Prussian military caste's idea of honor is repudiated as nothing but "vanity and capriciousness," based not on an inner sense of personal integrity, but rather "dependent on the most fickle and arbitrary thing that exists, judgments of society built on quicksand" (HF I/1, 679–80).

In its final place, Victoire's letter, I believe, does not so much contravene the preceding document as offer a personal enlargement and corrective of it. In any case, the two letters are by no means mutually exclusive; both approach the truth—and differing truths at that—without necessarily reaching it.

Its historical setting notwithstanding, this psychological analysis of the breakdown in Prussian esprit more than 75 years earlier had obvious implications for the blood and iron society of the Second Reich in which a heady sense of invincibility built upon militarism prevailed at every level of society. It is one of Fontane's major themes. Closely related to *Cécile,* as well as *Irrungen, Wirrungen* and *Effi Briest* in its treatment of rigid and unthinking adherence to an ossified code of honor and acceptance of a caste superiority by no means obsolete in Fontane's Prussia, *Schach von Wuthenow* was both historical commentary and a contemporary cautionary tale. Moreover, as we have seen, it represented the first full flowering of Fontane's literary techniques. With it his career as a significant writer of German fiction really began.

Chapter Four
Wilhelmine Portraits: Good Prussians All

With the appearance of *L'Adultera* in 1880, Fontane began the series of novels of contemporary life in the Second Reich upon which his fame securely rests. Beginning with the period shortly after the establishment of the empire and continuing almost up to the year of the author's death in 1898, they chronicle the cultural, economic, moral, and social evolution of the Reich's first three decades. Although almost every level of German society in the era is touched upon, the primary focus remains on the upper classes, specifically the lower ranks of the military aristocracy, the Prussian *Schwertadel,* and the rich bourgeoisie. Several stories also explore the world of the German petit bourgeois, still involved in handwork and maintaining a sense of middle-class pride that separates them from the faceless masses of the industrial work force then thronging to Berlin. It has been pointed out that in his depiction of the everyday life of this broad group ranging from the lower nobility and bourgeois to the lower middle classes, Fontane opens a new social realm for the novel, going a good deal beyond English writers like Jane Austen and Thackeray, who were in many respects his predecessors in the presentation of upper class society.[1]

By and large, however, except in supernumary roles—and sometimes then with telling symbolic effect—the Berlin proletariat or the rural peasantry do not assume center stage in Fontane's novels. Despite the sympathy with the industrial working classes which he had revealed years earlier in his translations of English worker poets, Fontane the novelist leans toward the presentation of those levels of German society in which he himself circulated and knew first hand, where cultivation, sophistication, witty conversation, and good taste set the tone.

Thus, although an unblinking realist, whose eye for detail and ear for linguistic nuance set him apart from his contemporaries, Fontane is no naturalist or scientific determinist; proletarian tragedy is not his purview and the winds of heredity and environment do not blow through the pages of his novels. The free will of his chief characters is also very much in evidence. Overall he depicts individuals consciously in conflict with their social order. Adding a particular piquancy is the recognition by most of his figures in crisis that the social order with which they collide, although intuitively understood to be transitory and limited in the larger sense, seems somehow immutably right in the narrower view. Good Prussians all, Fontane's characters generally accept their society and do not seek to alter it.

Northeastern regions of the empire, primarily the capital and its outlying regions, are the setting. A few stories go as far afield as the Baltic coast or the favorite summer haunts of the Berlin bourgeoisie in the Harz Mountains to the west, or Silesia in the east. Thus, with few exceptions, all the novels take place in an area of which Berlin is the center, ranging no more than 100 miles in any direction. It is above all Brandenburg Prussia, as absorbed into the Reich while retaining a substantial portion of its identity, that is portrayed, and except for a few caricatures, it is Prussians who people the pages of Fontane's finest novels.

Discounting *Schach von Wuthenow*, which also takes place in Berlin more than a half century earlier, these stories indirectly chronicle the evolution of the city since the founding of the empire. In roughly chronological fashion and with enough realism to permit an observant reader to follow its growth, Fontane shows Berlin as it expands almost from book to book.[2] Thus earlier novels such as *L'Adultera* still show the rich with summer villas just beyond the edge of the Tiergarten; the metropolitan area has hardly passed west of the Brandenburg Gate. In *Irrungen, Wirrungen,* which takes place only a few years later, however, what is soon to become the center of fashionable West Berlin, the crossing of the Kurfürstendamm and Kurfürstenstraße, is still the location of a truck garden, and Wilmersdorf still an outlying village. Botho's bachelor quarters in the Bellevuestraße and his apartment with his wife somewhat farther west in the Landgrafenstraße mark the rapid growth of the new capital westward beyond the confines enclosed by the Brandenburg Gate. In *Der Stechlin* (The Stechlins), members of the nobility ride municipal horse cars from one part of the city to another, and asphalt is being laid on its streets. The era of imperial Berlin under Wilhelm II is under way.

L'Adultera

Conceived in December 1879 and completed by the spring of 1880, *L'Adultera* was serialized in the magazine *Nord und Süd* the same year.

Because of the new work's somewhat dubious moral nature and the relatively modest success of both *Vor dem Sturm* and *Grete Minde,* Fontane was unable to come to an agreement with his regular publisher, Wilhelm Hertz, and finally offered the novel to the Breslau publisher Salo Schottländer under whose imprint it appeared in March 1882.

Although inferior to *Schach von Wuthenow, L'Adultera* is nevertheless a milestone in Fontane's evolution. Based on a situation that had occasioned a great deal of gossip in Berlin only six years before, it represents his first published utilization of contemporary material. In 1874, Therese Ravené, 22 years younger than her industrialist husband, deserted him for a young banker from the East Prussian city of Königsberg. The affair caused a sensation, especially when Louis Ravené agreed without protest to a divorce. Within several years the lovers married and embarked on a new life in the provinces, where they raised a large family. Louis Ravené died in 1879, the year Fontane began his work.

In creating a work from a scandal still fresh in the public mind, Fontane did not deviate essentially from the practice he had begun with *Grete Minde,* and which by now had become the matrix of his fiction: the psychological study of an individual whose transgression against accepted moral, ethical, or social standards has led to general exclusion and condemnation. By shifting from the historical to the contemporary scene, however, he made the most significant advance of his career. *L'Adultera* represents the transcendence of antiquarian romanticism in favor of a realism hitherto unknown to the German reading public.

The highly developed skills of a journalist as well as a careful eye kept on Berlin society over many years had obviously honed Fontane's talents. With a reporter's sense for the facts, he also did not shrink from employing particulars from the original cases whenever they met his requirements. Suggested no doubt by the auction notice from the autumn of 1879 found among the author's notes, Louis Ravené's art gallery and his collection of tropical plants, for example, provided useful elements in *L'Adultera.* Moreover, mutual acquaintances evidently provided the writer with details sufficient to make the novella's origins clear to those who had long memories, so that on 27 April 1894, almost 15 years after writing the story, not for the first time Fontane felt compelled to refute charges that in the realism of his depiction he had committed an indiscretion. "I never entered the Ravené house," he asserted, "and I saw the beautiful young woman but one time in a box at the theater, the husband only once at a London social gathering, and the lover (a business trainee named Simon) absolutely never."[3]

First among the risks in the choice of a current topic was the moral factor. It was one thing to depict dubious behavior in an historical context, quite another to present it as contemporaneous in the rigidly caste- and morality-conscious society of Wilhelmine Germany. With *L'Adultera,* the 60-year-old writer held up a mirror to his age, revealing an image it would have preferred not to behold. On more than one occasion he was to suffer for the clarity of the reflection he presented.

To be sure, Fontane's variant of the age-old tale of seduction and adultery is scarcely a dramatic story of grand passion. Passion and sexual intimacy—never the author's forte—are discreetly and somewhat clumsily circumvented, and readers left to draw their own conclusions. Nevertheless, by the standards of Germany in the 1880s, *L'Adultera* counted as a highly inflammatory book. Depicting a violation of the marital code was scandalous enough; also flouted in its pages, however, was society's expectation that the guilty be condemned. Although ostracized from Berlin society and bereft of her children by her first marriage, no small price, to be sure, Melanie van der Straaten is nevertheless not presented as suffering unendurable punishment for her serious breach of the moral code. Indeed, she transcends society's punitive efforts, and the book concludes with what was for its time a morally highly problematic happy ending.

With regard to the ending, in a letter written on 5 May 1883, Fontane revealed another basic principle of his approach to fiction that indicates how far he had come from the conventional moralistic ethos dominant in much of the Reich's literature. The author's task, he argued, was not didactic but objective reporting and analysis of the reality he found. Therefore, he held that *L'Adultera* presented "a piece of life, without any secondary intention or tendentiousness."[4] To a critic's argument that literature should show moral transgressions punished, he replied, "If art is supposed to maintain or improve the moral condition, then *you* are right. If art is simply supposed to reflect life, then *I* am right. I only desired the latter. The story happened just that way and the lady involved sits to this very day, beloved and respected, surrounded by a pack of brats up in East Prussia."[5]

Fontane's version of events is a simple one. In the Berlin of the boom and bust years following the establishment of the Reich, a young woman of 27, married for a decade to a rich financier 25 years her senior, slips into an affair with a younger man. Pregnant, she abandons husband and children for a new life. She and her lover flee to Italy, where, after receiving word of her divorce, they marry and she bears a child. Returning to Berlin, she is ostracized by society at large and rejected by her children. Her new husband's business failure enables her to take the consequences of her act upon herself in rebuilding their lives. At the end she receives a token of forgiveness from her first husband.

As is to be expected, a great deal about the life of the well-to-do in the years after the founding of the Reich is revealed. The van der Straatens own not only a comfortable apartment in central Berlin but also a summer villa on the edge of the city's large park, the Tiergarten. There, scarcely an hour's stroll into the suburbs, Melanie spends the warmer part of the year in luxurious surroundings, replete with a grand piano, elaborate gardens, and a palm house modeled after the famous topiary at Kew. Throughout the year the family leads a comfortable, regular life, embellished by travel, dinner parties, art, and music.

Fontane also employs the cultural forces of the age for his own purposes. The epoch's most significant and provocative figures, Bismarck and Wagner, serve as the subjects of dinner conversation as part of the realistic desideratum of the novel. The diatribe of one of the van der Straatens' dinner guests, Dusquede, offers insight into the distrust with which the Iron Chancellor's political pragmatism was viewed by the older Prussian aristocracy. But its primary function is to set the stage for what proves to be far more significant within the context of the story, the discussion of Wagner. Superficially, van der Straaten's tirade against the Bayreuth Master reflects the intensity of contemporary feeling engendered by Wagner, most radically formulated, of course, in Nietzsche's repudiation of his former mentor in the late 1880s. In *L'Adultera* Fontane utilizes the Wagner controversy to underscore the rift between husband and wife. Thus Melanie's husband strikes a frequently heard note in his characterization of Wagner's music as a form of witchcraft. His specific rejection of the "Tannhäuser und Venusberg-mann" (HF I/2 33), which makes clear that the eroticism of Wagner's music is particularly abhorrent to him, uncovers a subtle tension between him and his young wife. As is to be expected, Wagner's "witchcraft" suffuses nearly every moment of the relationship between Melanie and her lover Rubehn. Not only does mutual regard for Wagner create a spiritual bond between them that excludes van der Straaten, but its very nature confirms them as acutely sensitive to the eroticism that Melanie's husband repudiates. Similarly, the tropical humidity of the palm house in which they succumb to their passion is not only redolent of associations with Goethe's *Die Wahlverwandschaften,* as the chapter title suggests, but also of the atmosphere of lascivious decadence of Richard Wagner's world.

Fontane was essentially amusical and certainly no Wagnerite—in a fit of claustrophobia at Bayreuth in 1889 he fled the darkened theater before the end of the prelude to *Parsifal*—but as this work makes evident, the critic and alert cultural observer was quite familiar with the outlines of Wagner's works and was able to employ them effectively in the novel. At Rubehn's and Melanie's first encounter, for instance, "Wotan's Farewell" is heard in the background. As Rubehn pauses in his conversation, a bond between him and Melanie is established. The Wagner excerpt seems chosen scarcely by chance. As those familiar with it know, this extract from *Die Walküre* ends with a warning, thundered out to the Siegfried motif, that no one may approach the sleeping Brünhilde who fears the spear of Wotan. Van der Straaten's age makes the combination Wotan, Brünhilde, Siegfried/van der Straaten, Melanie, Rubehn a likely one, especially since we have learned that the newcomer is himself a modern Siegfried who wears the Iron Cross for courage displayed on the battlefield. Similarly, it seems more than coincidental that at the moment Melanie, like Sieglinde in the first act of Wagner's music-drama, bestows on Rubehn her special nickname, with subtle Old Testament associations concerning the possibilities of their relationship, she instructs her friend Anastasia to break a branch from one of van der Straaten's ash trees, announcing that "We can call it the Rubehn-ash" (HF I/2, 72). Wotan's spear, as alert Wagnerians including Rubehn know, is hewn from the mythical world ash tree stem and is ultimately destroyed by Siegfried, the hero who knows no fear. The fact, moreover, that the individuals involved are members of the Jewish bourgeoisie makes Fontane's utilization of one of the most famous works of the notorious Bayreuth anti-Semite a striking anticipation of Thomas Mann's parody of the identical work in *Wälsungenblut* (Blood of the Wälsungs) a generation later. Naturally, other Wagnerian associations, Tristan-Isolde-King Mark or Hagen-Siegmund-Sieglinde, are also never far below the surface, and van der Straaten's pointed references to them contribute unremittingly to the process of estranging his wife.[26]

In Melanie's boorish yet sympathetic husband, Fontane not only created his first full-dimensional Berliner and bourgeois caricature; he also registered his most complete psychological success to date. Van der Straaten's rudeness, his tactlessness and proclivity for outrageous Berlinisms, as well as his self-satisfied rejection of the conventions of seemly behavior, combine with a positively self-destructive sense of fatalism to practically force his wife from him. The arrival of a copy of the Tintoretto painting after which the novel is titled, interrupting an episode of apparent domestic tranquillity, is more than a somewhat heavy-handed foreshadowing of events. It is the first of an entire series of provocations that drive Melanie into Rubehn's arms. Boorishness, demonstrated time and again, whether at dinner or during an outing, especially after the arrival of the sensitive and tactful house guest, make their estrangement almost inevitable. Even van der Straaten's last-minute offer of reconciliation, a half-facetious trivialization of his wife's adultery as the repetition of an age-old situation, violates in Melanie's eyes the individuality of her act, and closes the door for good on any hope of conciliation.

Admittedly, to the extent that he succeeds in portraying the wronged husband, Fontane is less successful in presenting the adulteress herself. For all the subtle traits of personality suggested both by the action and through symbolic connotation, he leaves perhaps too much to the reader—such as the intensity of Melanie's aversion to her husband and her attraction to Rubehn. Problematic for other reasons is her rehabilitation. Her long scene with van der Straaten in response to his kindly meant but clumsy willingness to overlook what she has done is contrived to make clear that she and no one else accuses herself and exposes her transgression to the world: "I want to leave," she tells her husband, "not because of guilt but because of pride . . . so that I can rehabilitate myself in my own eyes. I can't bear the demeaning feeling any longer that is associated with all these lies. I want to have things clear again and hold my head up again. And I can only do that if I go, if I separate from you and openly admit to the entire world what I've done" (HF I/2, 101).

In cutting her ties to her former life, Melanie is not unlike Ibsen's Nora, with whom she has often been compared. Yet, unlike Ibsen's figure, she has by no means severed all bonds. Her new life stands under the protection of another man and together they seek reintegration into the same society whose moral code they have flouted. To be sure, in a final contrivance, the collapse of Rubehn's business blunts the argument that Melanie has merely exchanged one form of comfortable existence for another. Coming on the heels of her rejection by her children and fear of losing Rubehn, it is for Fontane the only possible means of ratifying her decision, her absolute commitment to the new existence she has chosen for herself. Yet it remains a somewhat dubious method of convincing the reader of the depth of her commitment to her new husband, otherwise more spoken about than anywhere depicted. In a sense, *L'Adultera* is actually two stories, the first portraying the estrangement of Melanie from her husband, the second presenting her renewal. Fontane obviously succeeded far more effectively at the first.

Other flaws are easy to find. The psychological path to adultery proves far more fascinating to the author than that of social reintegration. Rubehn, the man for whom Melanie has sacrificed everything, overwhelmed in the first two-thirds of the book by the ebullient van der Straaten, scarcely acquires dimension even toward the end. Indeed, there is more than a modicum of truth to Demetz's allegations (Demetz, 155) that the author's interest seems to wane as soon as van der Straaten disappears, and that in the Christmas tree sentimentality of the happy ending, Fontane slips perilously close to unvarnished kitsch. Similarly, a number of scenes, including the arrival of the painting depicting the biblical "woman taken in adultery" as well as the ensuing announcement of Rubehn's arrival as house guest, not to mention his unexpected skill at catching a ball, are not without a certain measure of heavy-handed contrivance.

It is clear that *L'Adultera* stands in the shadow of the finer works that followed. At the same time, its value as Fontane's first investigation of the conflict between the individual and the code of contemporary values cannot be denied. Moreover, with this work Fontane truly discovers his theme and the milieu most suited to his genius. Granted that it is a transitional work whose psychological nuances are neither so profound nor so finely wrought as what was to come, yet *L'Adultera*, merely as a social chronicle, the first of the stories dealing with Bismarck's Berlin, remains a viable document of the life of the elite in the newly founded German Empire.

Cécile

Critics are scarcely of a single mind regarding the second of Fontane's novels to deal with life in the Reich. An example of the author's ability to combine unrelated events into a story, the work's origins go back to an outline penned between 1877 and 1879 as part of the fragmentary novel *Allerlei Glück* (All sorts of happiness). For the latter,

Fontane had sketched the paramour of a German prince, who after his death is married off by his successor. Combined with this character type was an incident involving the son of Count Philipp zu Eulenberg, who, on informing his commander of his intent to marry a woman of questionable reputation, was told, "One makes love to such ladies but does not marry them." Challenging his superior for the insult to his fiancée, he was court-martialed and sentenced to two years of military imprisonment although soon pardoned by the emperor. These elements were blended to form the principal action of *Cécile* (1887). By reversing the roles so that it is not the junior officer but the senior who extends the challenge, Fontane created a chain of events that permitted no evasion of the outcome circumvented in reality.

For a location where a low-ranking officer might without breach of decorum come into contact with a retired colonel and his wife, the author resorted to Thale, a resort in the Harz Mountains much favored by the Prussian upper-middle classes, and a spot Fontane regularly visited, first in 1868 and then throughout the early 1880s. The symbolic possibilities of its local sites and the fluidity of social interchange it offered determined Fontane's visit in 1884, while he was preparing the novel. The Hotel Zehnpfund, where he stayed, became the setting for the first part while personalities encountered there, above all the attractive and nervous wife of the court preacher Strauß, contributed to the cast of the evolving work, which crystallized on a three-hour woodland walk on 19 June 1884. *Cécile* was serialized in the periodical *Universum* from April until September 1886. As an indication that Fontane did not yet enjoy a commanding position among contemporary writers, however, two publishers, including Hertz, who had printed the *Wanderungen* and several fictional works, declined the novel, which was finally published in the spring of 1887 by the house of Emil Dominik.

"A brash young fellow, 35, man of the world, loves and worships— no, worships is too much—loves and pays court to a beautiful young woman, ailing, appealingly provocative. One fine day she turns out to be the former paramour of a prince. Immediately a change in tone, importunate advances combined with the attitude of being perfectly justified. Conflicts, tragic outcome." Thus Fontane described the plot of *Cécile* to a prospective publisher.[7] Based on the moral ethos of nineteenth-century German aristocratic society, interwoven with a strongly fatalistic tendency, the story is, however, not as simple as described. The "brash young fellow," the former Prussian officer von

Gordon, newly returned from abroad, becomes acquainted with a beautiful woman and her solicitous but aloof husband, a retired colonel, at a resort. Cécile St. Arnaud's lack of formal education, as well as her sensitivity, combined with a naive responsiveness to attention, add to her fascination. Unable to fathom her mystery, Gordon writes his sister, but is called away before receiving a response. Some time later, he renews the acquaintance in Berlin, falling increasingly under the spell of the enigmatic woman who in the city appears more the woman of the world. Yet her religious scruples, nervous sensitivity, and solitary way of life continue to mystify him. His sister's letter clarifies everything. Cécile is the former paramour of a princely house; her reputation had led officers of her husband's regiment to protest his marriage, leading to the death of a subordinate in a duel. Now she appears to Gordon in a different light. Almost perversely, he becomes provokingly forward in his conversation and is warned of the peril he courts. Efforts to escape are thwarted; he leaves Berlin but is brought back by duties. Unexpectedly he encounters Cécile coquettishly bantering with an admirer. A mixture of indignation and jealousy drives him to confront the pair. Called to account, von Gordon falls in the inevitable duel. Overwhelmed with guilt, Cécile takes her own life.

In *Cécile,* Fontane displays renewed mastery of the conventions of the novel of high society. Amusing conversation on balcony and veranda, outings, formal dinners, typical constituents of his fiction, make up the action. New, however, are representatives of the middle and artistic classes of Bismarck's Reich. A female painter, a retired parson, a caricature of a pompously boring German academic suggestively named Eigenhard aus dem Grunde function not only as foils for the chief figures but almost as a chorus, interpreting and commenting on the action. Most prominent are two bumptious Berlin vacationers who anticipate the outcome of the relationship of the St. Arnauds and Gordon by alluding to the murder at the end of Schiller's *Wallenstein's Death.*

St. Arnaud and Gordon, the principal male figures, are thoroughly Prussian aristocrats in bearing and demeanor. Because of his foreign experiences, Gordon is depicted as more objective, easygoing, and urbane. Yet as the younger, less experienced man, he remains narrowly opinionated in matters of morality. Befitting the professional soldier, St. Arnaud is cultivated, courteous, and correct, but at the same time almost sinister in his inflexible air of self-esteem based on his reputation as a man of iron will and honor. Indeed, although the tragedy is provoked by Gordon's insult to Cécile, it is in fact only the superficial cause. Fontane makes explicit that it is not simply defense of his wife's honor but rather the assault on his sense of self through the younger man's failure to take his reputation seriously enough that impels the elder man to act. Müller-Seidel (Müller-Seidel, 184) has rightly pointed out that *Cécile* is a novel in which the woman is reduced to the status of an object, a mere chattel of the men whose values are ultimately the cultural and moral determinants of the society.

Echoing Fontane, who argued that his story undertook "to depict a character which as far as my familiarity with novellas extends . . . has not yet been depicted,"[8] many critics, including Wandrey (Wandrey, 192), Fritz Martini,[9] and Müller-Seidel (Müller-Seidel, 186), have stressed the modernity of the title character, who in sensitivity and fragility seems drawn from the types favored by the next generation of impressionistic writers such as Arthur Schnitzler and Eduard von Keyserling. Cécile's dubious background obviously places her and her husband on the fringes of society. Yet her sensitivity and insecurity emanate not only from an inherently delicate nature but also from an existential awareness that she can never rehabilitate herself, neither before an implacable Wilhelmine moral rectitude nor before her own conscience, burdened as she is both by her past and by the blood that has been spilled because of her.

In addition to presenting a neurasthenic Magdalene-personality unlike any he had dealt with before, not since *Ellernklip* had Fontane written a work so steeped in fatalism. In the earlier work, traditional moral categories of crime and punishment, embellished with transcendental romantic trappings, held sway; in *Cécile,* it is the social code that becomes the means to the fulfillment of destiny. Moreover, on occasions the author expressed his intent to depict in *Cécile* a principle that could almost stand as the motto for a number of his later works: "Once someone gets in deep, regardless of [whether it is] through one's own guilt or an unfortunate combination of events, one never gets out. Nothing is forgotten."[10]

The story is thus interwoven with an underlay of adumbrations, leitmotivs, and symbolic allusions, all calculated to stress the inevitability of its outcome. Fontane drew above all on the fairy-tale associations of the Harz region, creating another *Antimärchen*. In it the legendary mountain area proves not to be the sort of enchanted realm Cécile hopes for when, on setting out from Berlin, she quotes the title of a popular novella by Fontane's friend Paul Heyse and characterizes her journey as a would-be "Reise nach dem Glück" ("A journey to happiness") (HF I/2, 144). In a related episode during an excursion into the mountains, she and her friends pass a villa that she delightedly compares to an enchanted castle in which peace and happiness must dwell. Gordon informs her that the house is instead a place where fulfillment was never found, and that its most recent owner had shot himself there. In another situation illustrative of the negation of the traditional fairy-tale happy ending that permeates the book, Gordon explains to Cécile that the Harz area is famous for witches, who "are in fact a local product and grow like red foxglove everywhere on these mountains" (HF I/2, 165). To the comment of the painter Rosa, that such an insight might be a warning, he jauntily responds that happy endings are the rule and reminds her of the maiden who always escapes her pursuer by leaping across a gorge. It makes a difference, counters Rosa, if the maiden is pursued or if a dangerous but beautiful princess pursues the knight: "A poor maiden, princess or not, always gets helped. . . . But when a knight and cavalier is pursued by a dangerous and beautiful princess or even just a dangerous and beautiful witch, which sometimes is one and the same, heaven doesn't do a thing, but just calls down its aide toi-meme. And that's as it should be. After all, cavaliers belong to the stronger sex and have the obligation to help themselves" (HF I/2, 166).

It is typical of Fontane's closely managed interweaving of such elements that the entire exchange foreshadows Gordon's fate, even to details such as the foxglove, which Cécile uses in her last meeting with him, or Rosa's warning "Nehmen Sie sich in acht" ("Take care"), which echoes again as he descends from the coach to enter the opera house for the unexpected and fateful meeting with Cécile.

Despite such artistic felicities, the response to *Cécile* has been mixed. Although Helmuth Nürnberger holds that the work shows Fontane at the beginning of his mastery,[11] others such as Lukacs and Demetz have had little positive to say for it, relegating it, chiefly because of its treatment of a relatively sensationalistic and peripheral problem, to the realm of the inconsequential literature of an effete era. Both views are correct. In the interplay of allusion, adumbration, and symbolism, *Cécile* is a work of substantial achievement. Yet despite subtle psychological touches and structural ingenuity, as with its immediate predecessor, *Graf Petöfy* (Count Petöfy), its narrow concern with scandalous aspects of the life of the nobility means its characters scarcely touch us. As a document of the social mores of upper classes in the Second Reich, it is not without its fascination, yet, if anything, these only emphasize the vastness of the gap separating contemporary readers from that gilded age rather than the similarities binding us to it.

Irrungen, Wirrungen

After nearly ten years before the public as a novelist, and after almost as many stories enjoying a critical but limited public esteem, *Irrungen, Wirrungen,* serialized in the summer of 1887 in the *Vossische Zeitung* (Voss's News), the liberal Berlin daily for which Fontane had been theater critic for more than a decade and a half, finally secured for the 68-year-old writer a substantial measure of literary fame. The reasons are obvious. Although there is no evidence to suggest that the story is based on a specific situation, it is permeated with the Berlin milieu and deals with an acute moral problem of the day in masterly fashion.[12] Not the first Fontane novel to feature the contemporary Prussian-German social order, it nevertheless posed its moral and social questions in such a clear-cut fashion, personified in such winning characters, that they could not be overlooked. Moreover, from an artistic viewpoint, it presented the full flowering of Fontane's realism. With this novel, published in book form in 1888, everything came together, the "great" Fontane had arrived.

Dating probably to December 1882, the manuscript was put aside several times in favor of other projects. It was not taken up again until early in 1884, when the author made several junkets around Berlin's environs to view sites that figure in the story, such as the Hinckeldey memorial, the St. James Cemetery, and the Rollkrug (a pub on the city's outskirts), and spent two weeks at Hankels Ablage (Hankel's Depot), a bucolic spot on the Spree a few miles southeast of the city.

Once again Fontane enriched a simple plot by the craft with which he presented it. A young Prussian aristocratic officer and a level-headed Berlin seamstress have fallen in love. Recognizing that marriage is out of the question, they yield to the inevitable, knowing that it will cost them their happiness. Accepting the role that society has designated for them, each marries as class dictates. So far the novel is scarcely more than a melancholy little tale, which in the hands of a less gifted writer in the sentimental 1880s might easily have become treacle. Fontane, however, instead of breaking off at the most nostalgically charged moment, continues by depicting the reality his protagonists are forced to choose, thereby subtly questioning a system in which the individual's rights are sacrificed to an inflexible yet already fossilized system of social values.

Structurally, *Irrungen, Wirrungen* is another variant of the typical Fontane model—the presentation of a situation and its consequences. The rising and falling action, with a clearly defined turning point near the middle, again occurs here. Characters and setting are vibrant. In his protagonists, the seamstress Lene Nimptsch and the cavalry lieutenant Botho von Rienäcker, as well as in Botho's chatterbox wife, Käthe, Fontane created some of his most unforgettable personalities. Even secondary figures, such as the irrepressible Frau Dörr and her penny-pinching husband, Lene's stepmother, Frau Nimptsch, and the man she ultimately marries, Gideon Franke, are all certifiable Berlin types. Yet apart from the clarity of its architecture and its winning characters, what also makes this work particularly fascinating is its richly spun web of leitmotivs, parallel situations, and symbols—in the author's words, "the hundred and, I can boldly say, the thousand nuances . . . I have imparted to this especially beloved work on its way through life."[13]

The novel is also packed with allusions to Berlin during its explosive growth as the center of the new empire. Botho comfortably characterizes his city as "probably one of the best of all possible worlds" (HF I/2, 350) while alternately admiring the Tiergarten, its main park, and the Brandenburg Gate, Berlin's most famous monument. Strolling down Unter den Linden, the city's central boulevard, he window shops in one of the exclusive galleries and dines with his uncle and a fellow officer at one of its finest restaurants. By the same token, Dörr's market garden lies across from the Zoological Gardens at the juncture of the Kurfürstendamm and Kurfürstenstraße, later to become the thriving center of West Berlin, while at the time of the novel one of several areas newly absorbed by the city to accommodate the thousands who flocked to its factories and shops. Thus, in addition to the work's poetic urgency, Berlin readers in the 1880s could not only recognize nearly every location in the novel, they could already look back with nostalgia to such spots as the inn at Hankels Ablage, which by the time of the book's appearance had burned down, replaced by a colony of villas, at one of which the author had written several chapters.

Moreover, not since *Schach von Wuthenow* had Fontane presented so probing an interpretation of the Prussian scene. The relatively effete problems of the aristocracy in *Cécile* or *Graf Petöfy* yielded to a more pressing and general topic: every individual's quest for happiness in a social scheme in which already obsolete criteria of class limited the possibilities of life fulfillment. A common practice of late nineteenth-century European society, the relationships of lower-class women with men of position, tacitly accepted as an outlet for the privileged, provided the background. For men in such affairs, discretion was the order of the day, and there was an unspoken understanding that no obligation existed; each gentleman was free to come—and go—as he pleased. At the same time, many women on the lower rungs of the social ladder had no choice but to resort to prostitution for survival. In less desperate situations, arrangements of the sort presented in the novel offered girls from the lower classes a chance to enhance a drab life with a bit of gaiety or glamour.

Yet while turning a blind eye to moral laxity among its upper-class men, Prussian society was by no means as liberal regarding their partners; the double standard prevailed absolutely. The Reich chastely regarded itself as a German-Christian state; its foundation was the German family and for that female virtue remained the unquestionable cornerstone. Shackled to the roles of wife and mother, women were unconditionally subordinate to their husbands, and liaisons outside marriage involved the peril of losing the primary middle-class virtue: respectability. As a number of figures in *Irrungen, Wirrungen* make clear, only through reintegration into the social scheme by marriage to a man willing to overlook her past could a woman regain a measure of lost esteem.

Fontane's treatment of this public secret was viewed by many as scandalous. The nobility took offense that such duplicitous games were portrayed as part of the young aristocrat's life-style; middle-class readers shared their outrage and bristled even more at the violation of their prudish sexual code. Under the banner of unbending respectability, aristocrats and bourgeois alike preferred to view such affairs as examples of the turpitude of lower-class women rather than as examples of the exploitativeness of gentlemen of rank or wealth. Subscriptions to the *Vossische Zeitung,* whose "better public" Fontane had hoped would be able to extract the "Berlinish flavor of the thing"[14] were canceled, the elderly author castigated. Nothing could better illustrate the tide of indignation than the infamous remark attributed to a member of the family of the newspaper's publisher, who during its serialization is reported to have sarcastically inquired, "Isn't that awful whore's story going to be over with soon?"[15]

In keeping with his tenet of presenting life as he found it, Fontane avoided the preacher's tone, refusing to pass judgment on the relationship of an aristocratic officer from a prestigious cavalry regiment with a seamstress. In a letter to his son Theodor, only a few weeks after the work's appearance, however, he took an unequivocal stand. While conceding, "that the world at large will not think as leniently about Lene as do I," he also argued, "that in this open commitment to a definite stand on these questions lies a bit of the value and a bit of the significance of this book. We are certainly up to our ears in every sort of conventional lie and should be ashamed of the hypocrisy we commit and the false game we are playing."[16]

The rules of the game are made evident early in the compositional scheme of the novel. Lene admits to her neighbor, Frau Dörr, that she harbors no hope of marriage to her handsome young man, who, violating regulations that officers always appear in uniform, pointedly wears civilian clothes when in her company, and takes her on walks and excursions to isolated areas, where they are not likely to meet anyone from his circle. The voluble and still attractive Frau Dörr, who argues that "it's still really better accord'n to the catechism" (HF I/2, 332), has also had a relationship with a nobleman, albeit strictly on a physical level. Her fate, being forced to marry whoever will take her, will be repeated by the younger woman. "Sure, it ain't much," admits Frau Dörr of her life with the penny-pinching old miser Dörr, "but it's still respectable, and you can still hold up your head anywhere" (HF I/2, 321).

Other aspects of the game lie in the nicknames employed by certain players.[17] Botho's explanation that they are merely in imitation of the imperial family is an embarrassed smokescreen. Between individuals of similar rank such names may be a harmless affectation; in relationships between aristocratic gentlemen and women of a lower rank, however, they have a more dubious role. Leveling social barriers, they facilitate sexual freedom. Equally important, they signify a lack of obligation for those who use them; real identies are not involved.

A further subtlety is implied by the names drawn from Schiller's *Die Jungfrau von Orleans* (*The Maid of Orleans*) that are used by Botho's comrades for their female companions. Inasmuch as the women do not understand the allusions to one of the great documents of German culture, the social and cultural superiority of their escorts is tacitly stressed. Equally significant, the names themselves are a constant double entendre, a piquant reminder that it is indeed a risqué game that is being played, a violation of a social taboo whose rejection offers amusement to all who knowingly participate. It is an indication of the genuineness of their relationship that Botho and Lene use true names with one another. But when Botho yields to the pressure of the moment to introduce Lene to his comrades and their lady friends in the same fashion, he reduces their love to the same sort of tawdry charade, a fact that becomes excruciatingly evident to Lene as later scenes unfold.

Certainly one of the reasons for the novel's enduring success has been its characters. In Lene Nimptsch, Fontane created the most sympathetic personality of his entire ouevre. Down-to-earth, uncompromisingly honest both with herself and others, intensely passionate and yet endowed with a charming naiveté, she stands with Goethe's Gretchen and Mignon as one of the great woman figures of German literature. Her relationship with an aristocrat is more than a mere sexual adventure or attempt to brighten an otherwise drab existence. Physical and ideal love are fused for Lene; her affair is the most profoundly enriching experience of her life and she willingly and knowingly accepts its consequences while explicitly exculpating her partner. Botho von Rienäcker, despite his inherent moral weakness, is scarcely less winning. A romantic who finds in the simpler lives of the lower classes and his love for Lene an idyllic respite from the sophisticated hollowness of his own world, he is nevertheless wholly dependent on the advantages accruing from his rank and never entertains giving up privileges Lene and her circle can scarcely imagine. It has been calculated that the gap between Botho and his seamstress mistress is so vast that Lene, who embroiders linens on a piecework basis for a concern that sells to the nobility, would have to work for 25 years to earn the sum Botho spends in one year as a bachelor officer.[18]

It is, of course, one of the ironic nuances with which Fontane has endowed *Irrungen, Wirrungen* that Botho's wife, Käthe, turns out to be exactly the type of woman he can scarcely abide and that his mocking description of a trip to Dresden is realized on his honeymoon. Käthe von Sellenthin is another of the novel's well-wrought figures. Spoiled, superficial, frivolous, unremittingly cheerful and "silly," as one of Botho's comrades characterizes her, almost a caricature of the primping, shopping, gossiping socialite, she unerringly functions as a perfect counterfoil to Lene. Her trivial nature notwithstanding, Käthe is not, however, a complete fool. Aware of her limitations, she cunningly turns them to account. In a pointed negation of Ibsen's *A Doll's House*, she recognizes and unhesitatingly accepts her role as Botho's "doll" (HF I/2, 466). Yet in her superficiality she is no partner for Botho. As Martini (Martini, 776) points out, "behind the mask of happiness that Botho wears in his socially acceptable marriage, sterility and lonely melancholy lie hidden." Indeed, it is a powerful symbol of the decay of the nobility as a whole and of Botho's future in particular that his marriage to Käthe remains without issue, so that while the House of Rienäcker's present existence has been assured, its future is by no means certain.

Other members of the Prussian nobility are delineated with a mixture of bemused skepticism and realistic objectivity. The existence of Botho's comrades is framed by the barracks and the gaming table. Used to a life of privilege, they combine insight and cynical wit as well as a certain ingenuity in exposing the frailty of Botho's hope of keeping his two worlds apart. Similarly, his uncle, von Osten, is a wonderful portrait of the old-fashioned Prussian Junker, starkly conservative, obstinate and rigid in his thinking, outspoken and blunt, and yet not without a certain honest charm. Von Osten's apoplectic tirade against Bismarck represents one of the novel's humorous high points; at the same time, it brings into focus the complexities of the domestic policies of the Iron Chancellor.

Subtle touches add to the picture of life in the Second Empire. Käthe's trip to Schlangenbad affords Fontane the opportunity to suggest the ways of the idle rich in a fashionable resort. Her description of an encounter with the rich Jewish banker's wife from Vienna and her daughter, who gorges herself on sweets, is not without undertones of anti-Semitism. Yet it also serves to show the snobbish sense of superiority displayed by the titled aristocracy towards its parvenu challengers from the bourgeoisie. Here too one of the significant motivating factors of the novel is deftly reinforced: the decline of the feudal nobility as an aristocracy of capital gradually displaces it as the dominant force in the social order. Indeed the encounter in the enclosed compartment of a train between the Prussian baroness and the Viennese Jewess is itself symbolic of the age. It is not without significance that Frau Salinger is en route to the same health resort as Käthe, to provide, no doubt, for a male heir. Does Fontane seem to suggest—and not without a certain malice—that, despite the greedy little imp who accompanies the lady, even the family fortunes of the up-and-coming bourgeoisie are, like those of the nobility, already in inevitable physical decline?

At the other end of the social scale stand the figures grouped around Lene. Notwithstanding her inherently comic qualities as a busybody counterfoil to the lachrymose Frau Nimptsch, and apart from her role as a parallel to Lene, Frau Dörr's naive bluntness and lack of discretion in matters of a sexual nature highlight the younger woman's sensibilities. Whereas it was clearly Frau Dörr's physical attractions that had captivated her nobleman lover, it is Lene's good sense and character that set her off for Botho. Yet in an ironic crossing of personalities, Fontane also suggests that, regardless of her attributes, the older woman—who is ever ready to discuss her sexual experiences—has found little reward in them, whereas Lene, in whom sexuality seems to smolder just beneath the surface, is painfully embarrassed at their slightest mention.

Frau Nimptsch represents for Botho perhaps even more decisively than Lene does the lack of pretension of the lower-class world, where pedigree is unimportant, and the primary consideration is not *who* one is but simply *that* one is. The hearth she constantly tends and its boiling teapot convey sharing affection and constant welcome. At the same time, she also expresses a resigned sense of grasping at the few shreds of happiness that life in its brevity offers the underprivileged. "Child, it don't hurt anything," she tells Lene. "Before you know it, you're old" (HF I/2, 332). Her death is more than the sentimental outcome for an inherently sentimental character or an opportunity for the author to add to the general nostalgia that permeates the book; it functions inalterably to seal the past. Through Frau Nimptsch's death the simple and idyllic world in which Botho felt utterly at home is forever lost; no possibility remains of ever going back.[19]

In his willingness to overlook Lene's blemished past, Gideon Franke has similarities with the old gardner, Dörr. Yet continuing his dialectical treatment of character, Fontane sets the two poles apart. Dörr has been governed by a satyr-like sexuality; indeed, not only his wife's physical attractions but the very fact that she has had a sexual liaison with a nobleman have led him to disregard her tarnished reputation. Franke, on the other hand, resolutely chooses Lene solely on the grounds of her character.

Although appearing late in the novel, Gideon Franke is one of its most interesting figures. The religious zeal that has led him to found his own sect, his American past, and his proletarian nature all contribute to his independent thinking, enabling him to break the straitjacket of Prussian middle-class morality and accept Lene on the basis of her personal qualities rather than her past. By making Franke a religious zealot, Fontane puts his decision to marry Lene into high relief. Precisely because of his fundamentalism, marriage to a sexually compromised woman is not merely a matter of overcoming social restrictions, but of contradicting deeply felt religious tenets. Yet recognition of Lene's inherent character, supported by his own spiritual independence, enables him to transcend the restraints of orthodox dogma. His homegrown views on the sixth commandment, which leave Botho completely nonplussed, mark him as an individual prepared to value another not simply according to the letter of the law but according to its spirit as well. Although Botho feels constrained to hold fast to an outworn social code, Gideon Franke—aptly named as he is—is prepared to take a stand for a new morality, rooted in honesty, openness, and integrity. Gideon, events prove, is indeed better than Botho.

Yet despite Gideon Franke's readiness to take an independent stand, submission to society's order is nevertheless the cardinal principle throughout the novel. Indeed, unchallenged acknowledgment of this concept lends a fundamental melancholy to the story from the beginning. Although Lene accepts that there is no hope for her relationship with Botho, the latter indulgently attempts to repress reality for a while. Nevertheless, he is ultimately compelled to call himself to account. In a typical Fontane situation, an individual in crisis takes stock alone and in the process encounters symbolic reminders of his situation. Botho's ruminations before the memorial cross to von Hinckeldey represent a turning point in the book. Astute enough to recognize that the dead man had been a victim of an outworn class precept, Botho knows quite well the absurdity of such principles in a rapidly industrializing world. Nevertheless, he inevitably draws the lesson with which he has been indoctrinated: "that who we are determines our actions" (HF I/2, 405).

At the crux of *Irrungen, Wirrungen* is thus an old German problem: the rights of the individual versus the claims of the social whole. Without question it is the collective, the social order as stability, that carries the day in this novel. Botho's act represents resigned acceptance of a social system in whose historical justification he no longer fully believes. Exemplifying a principle firmly held by Fontane, that no individual is ever required to be a hero, the young nobleman is not about to alter it; he is not, as he tells himself, the man to "challenge the world and openly declare war on it and its prejudices" (HF I/2, 404). In choosing the path of "order," he consciously rejects the dictates of the heart for the sake of the collective of family and tradition, in the grimly pessimistic recognition that it is easier to choose the path most in keeping with one's origins than to deliberately invite conflict by contradicting them. Nor does he alter his views. Although he regrets the necessity of having to act as he has, several years later, after fully realizing the price he has had to pay, he nevertheless reiterates his stand when a fellow officer asks his advice. But he is not the only one. When Botho raises the question of the loss of personal happiness with Lene, her answer is equally without illusion: "Then we live without being happy" (HF I/2, 408).

Thus the primary principle according to which characters live their lives in this novel is ultimately that the wise accommodate themselves to the reality they are given. Indeed, in a response to an evaluation from the editor of the *Vossische Zeitung,* the author wrote "Yes, you've hit it splendidly. 'Social custom holds sway and has got to do so,' but that it has to is sometimes hard. And because things are as they are, it's best that we keep off and let sleeping dogs lie. And whoever ignores this bit of good old-fashioned common sense—I don't like to speak about morals, . . . gets a knock that will last for life."[20]

Irrungen, Wirrungen is without a doubt the single Fontane novel most filled with the atmosphere and characters of Berlin. Recognizable types appear throughout: postmen, cab drivers, servants, shopkeepers, kept women, and gardners. The long chat between Botho and the innkeeper at Hankel's Depot not only reveals the former's easygoing way with those who are considered his social inferiors, but focuses on the indefatigable love of the inhabitants of the imperial capital for the lake and forest landscape surrounding their city; Botho's conversation with the coachman as he rides out to visit Frau Nimptsch's grave turns on the conditions of running a hackney in the city. Even Käthe, as her comments on returning home from the cure reveal, is not immune to the distinctive qualities of the coarser side of Berlin humor.

To the alert reader the work is a gold mine of fine— sometimes less fine—strokes of the pen. Words, situations, and objects occurring early appear later in a wholly different light, functioning as skillfully integrated leitmotivs. The dandy rooster, for instance, ignominiously put to flight by a neighbor's dog early in the novel, prefigures Botho's ultimate weakness in the face of social pressure; the strawberry shared by Botho and Lene in Dörr's garden, subtly suggestive of the highly charged sensuality between them, is grotesquely recalled near the midpoint of the work as Balafré's paramour stoops to pick one for him.

The word *bound* occurs in a variety of contexts. Wreaths appear in various forms with contrasting functions. That which Botho promises Frau Nimptsch becomes a memorial not only to her but to all the happy hours he has spent in the circle around her and Lene. In another subtle irony, on the very day he places his wreath at Frau Nimptsch's grave Botho burns the one that ties him to her daughter. And Lene, who has already experienced a wedding of sorts following the wreath episode at Hankel's Depot, refuses to wear a bridal wreath on her marriage to Gideon Franke.

Fireworks, a favorite image employed by Fontane to connote passion, suggest the intensity and brevity of Botho's and Lene's summer romance. They appear anew in the weather-worn placards lining the road as Botho rides out to the cemetery where Frau Nimptsch is buried. In fact, the ride to the cemetery, which makes up a substantial part of chapter 21, is in the density of its allusions almost Wagnerian[21] as an extended recapitulative interlude before the denouement, in which a host of previously introduced elements are recalled, varied, and expanded. Party-snapper sayings are recollected in allusions to William Tell, and stonemasons' shops interspersed between firework placards call to mind the fragmented fallen angels' heads discovered by the lovers on an evening stroll, while underscoring the transitoriness of happiness through love. Emphasizing Botho's bitter and hopeless situation, the refrain he, Lene, and Frau Dörr had sung on the evening of their walk returns again, recapitulated by a shabby pair of street musicians, its last lines taken up by a serving girl who brings to mind the one Lene had seen polishing kitchenware on their last day of happiness together. In all, the episode represents one of the high points of Fontane's skill in weaving symbols and situations into a rich poetic tapestry, a skill he termed, in reference to Goethe's *Wilhelm Meister,* "the art of tying together, of establishing relationships, of forging links" (HF III/1, 466).

To be sure, there are those critics who find in such consciously wrought literary creations as this chapter more evidence of Fontane's skill at artifice than at art. Nevertheless, for most, *Irrungen, Wirrungen* remains one of the unchallenged masterworks of German realism.

Stine

Initially roughed out in late 1881, almost half a year before *Irrungen, Wirrungen,* which preceded it into print by almost three years, *Stine*

(*Stine*) had a complex publication history. On its completion in 1888, Fontane had qualms about the story's appropriateness for the family magazine to which he had promised it and sought release from the agreement. Other outlets, including the *Vossische Zeitung,* in which *Irrungen, Wirrungen* had appeared, evidenced little interest so that the disappointed author despaired of placing it, even advising his son, then starting out as a publisher, against taking the work. Indicative of his growing acceptance by the younger literary generation, it finally found a home in the weekly *Deutschland,* an offshoot of the naturalist movement, between 25 January and 15 March 1890. His father's reservations notwithstanding, Friedrich Fontane published the first book edition in April 1890.

Parallels between *Stine* and *Irrungen, Wirrungen* inescapably bind the two stories—to the detriment of the former, which actually represents Fontane's first thoughts on the topic. Berlin in the mid-1870s is again the setting, and the exploitation of poor women by members of the Prussian aristocracy once more the subject. The reader is introduced to Pauline Pittelkow, a widow who has been set up as a kept woman in an apartment on Berlin's north side by Count von Haldern. The entire first third of the book is devoted to a dinner party arranged by the count, who brings a friend and his nephew, Waldemar. At von Haldern's suggestion, Pauline's unmarried younger sister Ernestine (Stine) and a school friend, the actress Wanda Grützmacher, are also present.

In the second part, the relationship between Waldemar von Haldern and Stine, only hinted at in the earlier section, is developed. The young nobleman, whose life has been under an unlucky star, has never fully recovered from wounds suffered in the Franco-Prussian War. In Pauline's sister he believes he has found a kindred soul. Declaring himself ready to reject all privileges and to start anew in America, Waldemar reveals to his uncle his decision to marry Stine, hoping only that his uncle will bring the family to accept his decision. The seemingly liberal Count von Haldern proves unyieldingly opposed to a mésalliance in his own family. He rebukes Pauline for fostering the relationship and is astonished to discover that she too realizes the impossibility of such a union, and prefers that Stine marry within her class. Waldemar in the meantime puts his suit to Stine, who, although admitting her love, refuses to marry him. The differences between them, she argues, are too great and she recognizes he is not physically capable of creating the new life he imagines for them. Knowing her decision to be unalterable, Waldemar takes an overdose of sleeping powders. At his funeral only Stine is grief-stricken. Her unlikely recovery is left open.

Compositionally, *Stine* must be reckoned among Fontane's poorer efforts. Not to its advantage can it be considered the "real pendant, . . . in parts less good, in parts better,"[22] to the far more balanced *Irrungen, Wirrungen*. Introductory scenes, devoted to preparations for the soirée at Widow Pittelkow's and the event itself, although full of allusions to be developed later, are spun out at such a leisurely tempo as to take up over a third of the entire length, yet their breadth is hardly justified by relevance to the main plot. From the second third on, nearly everything is narrated with a terse economy not characteristic of Fontane's best fiction. The final chapter, devoted to Waldemar's funeral, returns to earlier motifs such as the funeral procession witnessed by Pauline's daughter, or the lovelessness of the von Haldern family, and sentimentally rounds them off. All in all, it is difficult not to feel that Fontane failed to expand salient elements of the story, either because he felt the obvious similarity to situations already treated in *Irrungen, Wirrungen*, or—no less likely—because, having covered similar ground, he found his chief characters and what became of them simply less interesting.

A particular point, for instance, is the utilization of nicknames, in this case from Mozart's *The Magic Flute*. Fontane's excuse that in writing *Irrungen, Wirrungen* he had forgotten the nicknames he had used in the incomplete *Stine* and therefore used the same device in the former is not particularly convincing.[23] Certainly he was aware of this gross self-borrowing by the time he got around to completing *Stine*. Unwillingness to sacrifice the motif of the parody of the Mozart duet "Bei Männern, welche Liebe fühlen" no doubt played a part, but it is an indication of his overall dissatisfaction with the work as a whole, I believe, that he did not make the effort to alter it.

More serious are the imbalances in characterization. By far the most interesting figure, and obviously the one for whom the author felt the most sympathy, is Pauline Pittelkow. A robust, no-nonsense person, tough, unsentimental, and honest, she is among his most successful Berlin portraits, wholeheartedly devoted to the Prussian ideal of a well-arranged society in which every thing and every one has a place. True, the exigencies of life have denied Widow Pittelkow a respectable place, but with a Berlin sense of fortitude she has learned to make the best of things. Even though she abhors her position as von Haldern's mistress, she accepts what she cannot change and the concomitant moral and social isolation with her dignity and self-esteem well intact. At the same time, she fiercely fights to protect the respectability of her sister. Only awareness of her cultural inferiority to her patron puts her momentarily on the defensive. Double entendres irritate her, not because of their possible salaciousness but because of the mockery and affront to her personal dignity that she perceives behind them. Face to face with Count von Haldern, she matches the nobleman with her own sense of class honor, which for her consists not in blue blood or outworn family tradition but in an unyielding belief that true merit lies in the rejection of all hypocrisy and self-deception. Pauline is one of Fontane's most successful lower-middle-class figures, of that there can be no doubt; she is resolute, sensible, irascible and yet admirable in her honesty and forthrightness.

Nevertheless, despite her merits, such detailed characterization of a secondary figure skews the focus to the detriment of the story as a whole, as Fontane was well aware. "For me the Pittelkow woman and the old count are the chief persons," he lamely admitted to a critic in 1890, "and their depiction was more important than the story. That should certainly not be the case and a real storyteller has to be more just to the story as such, but that simply isn't in me."[24] An insightful comment, it reveals to what extent psychology and the delight in characterization guided Fontane's pen.

Count von Haldern is well aware of the ephemeral nature of the Prussian social order and shares with Waldemar a sense of fighting a hopeless rearguard action against historical inevitability. He readily grants that the case for the nobility has neither moral nor social justification. The arguments Fontane puts in his mouth unequivocally reflect his own conviction that the Prussian nobility had run its historical course and that it maintained its position merely because the inertia of the Reich's social order prevented it from toppling. Indeed, one of the few points that distinguishes *Stine* positively from its more significant predecessor, *Irrungen, Wirrungen,* is the candid treatment of the sociohistorical realities on which both are based. A deft caricature of the situation occurs in the final scene of chapter 5, in which the group joins in the refrain from an operetta, "Nothing's left, for me there's nothing left,/ But my honor, and this aging head,"[25] while Pauline, standing behind the count, lightly beats time with her fingers on his balding pate.

Equally as undermining as the disproportionate strength of secondary figures in *Stine* is the chief characters' lack of vigor. Comparisons between Waldemar and his literary cousin Botho von Rienäcker are inescapable. Both are the weak offspring of a dying privileged class aware of its incipient demise. Sickliness, Gerhard Friedrich (Friedrich, 110) points out, makes Waldemar less a representative of his caste than an individual case. Yet the argument could also be made that the sickly Waldemar is the perfect representative of his moribund caste. In any case, his illness makes the younger Haldern more desperate than Botho; having never known happiness, he perceives his only chance for it with Stine. Rejection by Stine leaves him completely defeated in his attempt to master reality, caught in a life in which he can find no hope for happiness, symbolized in the half-circles he draws and interprets in the sand (HF I/2, 556).

Fontane's efforts to motivate his tale in a psychologically credible fashion led him to apply the brush perhaps too thickly. Waldemar is portrayed as hopelessly doomed from the outset. Dismissed by Pauline as "a poor, sick chicken" (HF I/2, 506), he is presented as always having had a disposition towards suicide, as his cache of sleeping powders makes clear. An ailing and sensitive romantic, languidly relishing sunsets, "half in love with easeful death," he is the most decadent male figure in the Fontane menagerie. There is no mistaking him as one of those Germans who, by way of Novalis and the necrophilic atmosphere of certain works of Wagner, trace their lineage back to Goethe's *Werther,* to be ultimately celebrated by Thomas Mann in the likes of Gustav von Aschenbach and Hans Castorp. Indeed, through Waldemar and, to a lesser extent, its title character, *Stine* is infused with a sense of morbidity scarcely matched in German fiction until the creation of Hanno Buddenbrook.

As the author himself readily allowed, little positive can be said about the title figure either, especially when compared with her obvious parallel, Lene Nimptsch. "Stine as a figure remains far behind Lene. And, since she is the main heroine and gives the whole thing its name, the whole thing has to suffer along with it."[26] Essentially passive, Stine takes center stage only in two conversations with Waldemar. Neither contributes much to the rounding of her personality, and the first, a justification of her sister's way of life, merely reiterates ideas the author had expressed in Frau Dörr's comments in chapter 3 of *Irrungen, Wirrungen.*

Stine might be considered a better work if we did not have *Irrungen, Wirrungen,* with which it will always be compared. The superiority of the earlier work lies not only in its undeniable formal perfection but in its timelessness. In *Stine,* as a result of failing to expand his lovers beyond one-dimensional figures, Fontane resorted to sentimental cliché. *Irrungen, Wirrungen* continues to transcend its age precisely because in it the author rose above its lachrymose inclinations. Despite the vivid figure of Pauline Pittelkow, *Stine* fails, in part because it is poorly constructed but also because, lacking the cool irony characteristic of the author's best work, it remains too much a product of its maudlin and posturing age.

Frau Jenny Treibel

Written with *Effi Briest* and *Unwiederbringlich* (*Beyond Recall*) during the last years of the 1880s and the early 1890s and serialized in the *Deutsche Rundschau* from January through April 1892, *Frau Jenny Treibel,* Fontane's comic novel about the hypocrisy and snobbery of the Berlin bourgeoisie, is another of his unchallenged masterworks. The book, bearing the imprint 1893, was brought out in October 1892 by Friedrich Fontane's publishing house.

The psychological factor, as we have seen, had always been the driving impetus behind Fontane's narrative art. *Frau Jenny Treibel* is another landmark, however, because it marks Fontane's successful turning towards the investigation of specific personality types for their own sake. He had failed in this in *Stine* because the well-drawn Pauline Pittelkow was not the center of interest. In *Frau Jenny Treibel,* however, Fontane's delight in the presentation of characters blended perfectly with his slight but nevertheless delightful satire of bourgeois ostentation. Story and personages are an amalgam of circumstances, individuals, and episodes gleaned from his immediate family and acquaintances. The social aspirations of his wife, Emilie, whom he had known from childhood, in the same way as Professor Schmidt knows Jenny Treibel, no doubt contributed. So did the author's sister, Jenny Sommerfeldt, a Berlin pharmacist's wife whose pretensions her brother found alternately amusing and insufferable. Touches for Corinna were provided by his daughter Mete, while the "lovable egoist" (HF I/4, 461) Schmidt seems to be partly an ironic self-portrait. Much the same holds true of secondary characters. Through his sister, for instance, Fontane learned of other interesting bourgeois personalities such as a well-to-do industrialist's wife constantly at war with her own daughter-in-law. Like Jenny's daughter-in-law, Helene, the latter was also a stickler in matters of dress and a horror to her children's governesses, and had even sought to marry off a sister to another son of her husband's family. Other minor characters such as the Felgentreu family and the tenor Krola were also drawn from the author's social circle.

The novel describes a domestic tempest in a Berlin bourgeois family. As might be expected, wealth and ostentation are the gauges of social significance. The action is slight: Corinna Schmidt, an intelligent young professor's daughter, weary of genteel poverty, engineers her engagement to the son of her father's childhood friend Jenny Treibel. The latter has risen from modest beginnings in a grocery shop to become the wife of a rich manufacturer. With the hauteur of the nouveau riche, Frau Commercial Councilor Treibel rejects the marriage. Resigning herself to her fiancé's inability to break free of his formidable mother, Corinna calls off the engagement and accepts the other candidate, an academic like her father, who has been impatiently waiting in the wings. All dangers allayed, a reconciliation between the families follows at the wedding.

Fontane employs this modest plot to present ironic portraits of a number of types flourishing in the landscape of the newly created and pompously self-conscious Reich. While the author never made a secret of his admiration for the genteel charm of the old aristocracy, and also respected captains of industry for their willingness to take risks in pursuit of expansive goals, for the relentless social climbers of the new Germany he felt nothing but scorn. Apart from their sheer greed, particularly irritating to him was the eagerness of the newly arrived to display their wealth. Equally odious was their tendency to embellish their avaricious and patronizing ways with a sentimental patina of half-digested culture. The inherent inconsistency of relentless materialism paired with a smarmy avowal of high values he had found indigenous to the German character long before Bismarck's empire, if we are to believe the portrait of his master in pharmacy from his early days in Berlin (HF III/4, 185). But the boom years following the establishment of the Reich had been a particularly fertile period for such manifestations. *Frau Jenny Treibel* is thus the elderly writer's ironic monument to the driving pursuit of wealth and ostentatious display, the novel in which he sought to unmask "the hollowness, cliché-ridden emptiness, perfidiousness, effrontery, [and] hardheartedness of the bourgeois position, which talks about Schiller but means Gerson" [a Berlin department store].[27]

Yet despite the sharpness of his private judgments, in his fiction Fontane never sank to malicious satire or true social criticism. There is more satirical humor than vitriol in *Frau Jenny Treibel*. Its title figure is inherently comic and it is the transparent incongruity between her sentimentalized protestations of devotion to higher things and her decidedly pragmatic manner of acting that makes her rewarding.[28] The chief irony of the work is suggested in its subtitle, *Wo sich Herz zum Herzen find't* (*Where Heart Makes Way to Heart*). In this song, which she manages to sing at the end of her soirée, Jenny affirms her devotion to the uplifting poetic values acquired in youth. These have been gained, she gushingly assures Corinna in the first chapter, through contact with her father, Willibald Schmidt, from whom the poem had been a gift. Yet notwithstanding the sentiments of her favorite lyric, preventing heart from finding heart for the sake of gold is precisely what Jenny Treibel undertakes to do.

Her antics are met with roguish skepticism by her old friend Professor Schmidt, whose attitude toward Jenny is essentially that of the author's: whimsical acceptance of such a personality, which regardless of obvious failings is too fine a representative of the human comedy to be ignored. At the same time, Schmidt has no illusions. "She is a dangerous individual," he tells Corinna's would-be suitor, Marcel, "and all the more dangerous in that she herself doesn't really know and genuinely imagines she has a feeling heart and above all a heart 'for higher things.' But she only has a heart for all those things that can be weighed out, for everything that tips the scale, and bears interest" (HF I/4, 369f.).

Even though Jenny is the title character and it is her machinations that ultimately direct the action, Corinna is in many respects the primary figure. It is ultimately her fate that is decided and her character that is changed by the events the novel depicts. Her decision to marry Leopold Treibel is a conscious bid to turn her back on the narrow horizons offered by her father's way of life. "An inclination toward a life of luxury, which dominates the whole world these days, has me in its power too, just like all the others" (HF I/4, 344), she tells her disbelieving suitor-cousin, Marcel. Next to Lene one of Fontane's most delightful female personalities, like her creator, she is a conscious master of the adroit use of language. Her ensnarement of Leopold by flirtatiously playing up to the Englishman Nelson ranks among the novel's finest pages. Equally deft is her maneuvering of the feckless Leopold into a proposal; a step she later defends before his indignant mother as any woman's right to employ her wiles in an age that leaves the initiative in such matters superficially in the hands of the male (HF I/4,

447). In another fine touch, when she begins to recognize that she has lost the game, the usually talkative Corinna is reduced to savaging a roll and is compelled to yield to the wisdom of the family cook, Schmolke, who in warmth and solicitude represents Jenny's opposite.

But the novel's humorous criticism does not stop with satirical treatment of bourgeois hypocrisy. In the figure of Professor Schmidt, Fontane in part mocks his own occasionally self-indulgent ways while at the same time taking to task the oftentimes pompously self-important educated Prussian middle class, the so-called *Bildungsbürgertum*.[29] Thus although substantially more authentic than Jenny, Corinna's father is also caught up in his own world of delusion. More capable of meeting shortcomings, his own and those of life in general, through satire and irony, he is not above self-satisfied pontification and cultural exhibitionism, not to mention a certain unwillingness to make substantive personal commitments when needed. Bemused skepticism and a refusal to interfere characterize Schmidt's attitude to Corinna's choice of Leopold. His confidence is based, of course, on his conviction that Corinna's good sense and Jenny's character, which he knows only too well, will in the end carry the day. Wisdom it may certainly be, yet his readiness to permit things to run their course comfortably enables him to avoid giving his daughter support at a time when she could well use it. Informed of Corinna's betrothal to Marcel, he seems more enthralled at the prospect of gaining a colleague than by the prospect of his daughter's gaining a husband. At the same time, Fontane sees to it that Schmidt's role is not entirely passive. At the expedient moment, he steps in to encourage Marcel to make his move toward claiming Corinna as his bride, even though the young man must rein in his future father-in-law's enthusiasm for seeing to it that his daughter gets her comeuppance for having arrogantly overstepped her bounds.

If any figure in the novel may be described as genuine in the fullest sense of the word, it is less the relatively noncommital and teasingly skeptical professor than, as Kafitz has pointed out (Kafitz 87), his down-to-earth serving woman, Schmolke. Though superficially a traditional literary confidante, it is Schmolke to whom Fontane has imparted the majority of warmly humanitarian values. Thus it is Schmolke who brings Corinna to her senses in the crucial exchange in chapter 14 in which she makes clear to the girl that her obstinacy in continuing her relationship with Leopold is grounded not in love but in her stubborn desire to counter Jenny. Literarily related to Frau Dörr and Pauline Pittelkow, she is another example of the warmhearted common sense and innate nobility characteristic of the lower classes who frequent the edges of Fontane's novels.

In the Treibel men Fontane continues his list of nonheroes. Commercial Councilor Treibel, a literary cousin of van der Straaten in *L'Adultera,* is rich in contradictions and not at all without good points. Despite Jenny's accurate evaluation that "the prosaic weighs on him like lead" (HF I/4, 429), a healthy portion of ironic self-deprecation marks his personality. Yet ambition drives him into realms beyond his ken. His political misadventures under the aegis of the ludicrous monarchist-democrat Vogelsang, a grotesque parody of the eccentrics on the fringes of Prussian politics, are merely an opportunistic quest for added prestige, and reveal a crass misunderstanding of the democracy emergent in the late Bismarckian era. Although Treibel's defense of Corinna's and Leopold's engagement is decidedly on the mark, its logic proves ineffectual, for with an implacable determinism that contravenes Jenny's husband's better nature, Fontane stamps him as "the product of three generations grown ever wealthier in running factories." Thus, notwithstanding Treibel's intelligence and other good qualities, "with him as with his sentimental wife, the bourgeois element was deep in his blood" (HF I/4, 439).

Even more hapless is Leopold Treibel. Jenny's maternal grip has extinguished any spark of manhood in her weakling son. At Jenny's dinner, a play on masculine bravery associated with the Englishman Nelson's name is utterly lost on Leopold, who freely admits that he lacks any shred of heroism. His decision to sue for Corinna's hand is a desperate bid to liberate himself from his mother's grasp and to obtain through the daughter of Professor Schmidt a certain vicarious hold on self-reliance. His hopeless subservience to Jenny is, however, neatly suggested when, on the threshold of asserting his independence, he yields to the maternal admonishment concerning a second cup of coffee, and as he prepares to make his declaration to Corinna, he carefully puts his mother out of his line of sight.[30]

Structurally, the reader familiar with Fontane is again on well-trodden ground. Characters are delineated almost exclusively through conversational give-and-take. The exposition presents not one but two dinner situations, one at Treibels the other at Schmidts, that parallel each other internally. Excursions provide the mise en scène for turning points. Moreover, Fontane indulges his playful humor with a fairly large cast of secondary figures, many of them approaching caricature, to enrich the overall picture of upper-middle-class Berlin society in the late reign of Wilhelm I. Apart from the bizarre political agitator Vogelsang, two elderly aristocratic ladies from outermost court circles grace the Treibel table, providing a semblance of connection to throne and palace. The empire's growing role in international commerce forms the background of the episodes centering on the comically unprepossessing Englishman Nelson. Those surrounding Lizzi, the Treibel grandchild, done up like a doll princess to emulate her mother's Hamburg-grown ideal of an upper-class English child, underscore the preposterous ostentatiousness of the Wilhelmine bourgeoisie and their growing Anglophilism, which follows the lead of the court, as the stock of the heir apparent and his English wife, Victoria's daughter, seems to be on the rise.

The ending is problematic. Certainly, despite her machinations and obvious hypocrisy, Jenny Treibel does not seem to get the comeuppance she so richly deserves. Instead, following a reconciliation with the Schmidts, she appears to have won on all fronts. Yet who can believe that the final state of affairs will satisfy her for long? Like her husband's political campaign, her manipulations will prove to be nothing short of a disaster. To preserve her bourgeois superiority, she has been compelled to foster her son's marriage into a family she cannot abide. Moreover, the prospective bride, Hildegard, is scarcely the self-reliant and intelligent daughter-in-law Jenny has wanted for her son, and which, of course, Corinna would have been. Is there any doubt that Hildegard will nettle Jenny's Berlin sensibilities as much through her horsey Anglophilism and Hamburg airs as Helene has? With her advent, moreover, the power of the Hamburg Thompson-Muncks over the Treibels becomes absolute; not Jenny but they are the real victors. As a final touch, Jenny and her husband are now assured of even more primped and dandified "angels" like Lizzi to carry the Treibel name and fortunes into the future.

On the other side of the ledger, Fontane sees to it that Corinna Schmidt has been cured of unseemly pretentiousness. Jenny and all she stands for have been routed in the Schmidt household and Corinna has found her way back to her better self to end up marrying her cousin Marcel, who in the benign view of Schmidt and Schmolke has clearly been the right man all along.

Fontane's ironic use of name symbolism, something he frequently indulged in, is in *Frau Jenny Treibel* perhaps too much of a good thing. The surname Treibel derives from the German verb *treiben,* to urge or drive onward. Similarly, Fräulein Honig (Miss Honey), Jenny's companion, is an embittered old maid, Nelson, the English guest, an unheroic bumpkin, and the ladies Ziegenhals (Goatneck) and Bomst (suggesting a large bosom) diametric opposites of the connotations of their names. At the same time, the skeptical but more authentic professor is endowed with the unprepossessingly German name Schmidt, and the true representative of Berlin good sense answers to the utterly unpretentious name of Schmolke.

Overall, symbolic effects are less prominent in *Frau Jenny Treibel* than in many Fontane novels. Where they appear they are primarily ironic, for instance, Jenny's imperious position at her dinner table perched on an air cushion, or the thin voice with which the otherwise imposingly built socialite delivers her favorite song. Other effects, such as the Treibels' fountain, whose waters spray Corinna and her admirers Nelson and Leopold as Corinna is in the midst of setting her net for the latter, or the haughtily watchful cockatoo atop its bar and the yapping but tightly leashed household lapdog, also suggest the mistress of the household and those firmly under her control. Equally felicitous is the fact that the Treibel fortune rests on Prussian blue dye, associated with the underlying militarism of the empire. It is another of Fontane's ironic touches that Leopold is too weak in the chest to have earned full Prussian identity by wearing the family's product himself. His ultimate fate is itself symbolic, however, for although it is outwardly a male society in Fontane's novels, in *Frau Jenny Treibel* the bourgeois struggle for success is ultimately revealed to be in the hands of designing women.

Posthumous Addendum: *Mathilde Möhring*

Although not published during his lifetime, no work would seem to make the possibility of female dominance more evident than *Mathilde Möhring*, a short novel among the projects taken up by Fontane while still working on *Frau Jenny Treibel*. Not until 1906 was it serialized in the popular weekly *Die Gartenlaube*, in a version edited by Josef Ettlinger. This also appeared the following year as part of the volume *Aus dem Nachlaß von Theodor Fontane* (Posthumous works of Theodor Fontane). Two generations later, when the East German scholar Gotthard Erler compared the manuscript with Ettlinger's text, he discovered substantial differences. Chapter headings had been excised, words, phrases, and even sentences changed or deleted. What had been interpreted as *Mathilde Möhring* for six decades did not in fact correspond with what the author had left. Only in 1969 was an authentic version genuinely in keeping with the author's probable intentions made available by Erler.[31]

Relatively little is known of its genesis. Probably one of several projects begun in January 1891 and worked out in the following summer, *Mathilde Möhring* seems to have been put aside in September. Documentary evidence found on the back of a manuscript page of *Der Stechlin* definitely indicates it was again on Fontane's desk in 1896, to be pushed aside once more, this time in favor of the latter. Fontane's widow reviewed the manuscript in 1901, a year before her death, and proclaimed it unfit for publication.

References to the conflict between Kaiser Wilhelm II and Bismarck enable us determine that the story spans the two-year period from October 1889 through October 1891. Thus although focusing like *Irrungen, Wirrungen* and *Stine* on the lower-class milieu, *Mathilde Möhring* takes place almost 15 years later, as the Reich begins its third decade. Although not concerned with the conflicts that arise when personal interests cross class lines, a strong sense of class hierarchy nevertheless permeates this story, suggesting how deeply status and the urge toward upward mobility had penetrated Wilhelmine society even among the lowest strata. The quest for status is ultimately the driving force of the action, which shows how the unattractive but cunning Mathilde maneuvers a provincial bürgermeister's son, Hugo Großmann, who has taken lodgings with her and her widowed mother, into proposing, even though he considers her socially inferior. Recognizing that he lacks ambition or fortitude, Mathilde stipulates that she will marry Hugo only when under her tutorage he passes his preliminary law examination. Knowing that he does not have the talent for a career in city or national government, she steers him to a post as bürgermeister in a small town and there smooths his way by suggesting improvements he can easily propose while ingratiating them both with the local gentry. The Frau Bürgermeister's future seems assured until her husband unexpectedly takes ill and dies. Undaunted, Mathilde returns to Berlin and her mother and becomes a teacher.

The lower-class milieu portrayed in *Mathilde Möhring* underscores the author's kinship with his younger naturalist contemporaries. Had the story been published, it would probably have been enthusiastically hailed by them. At the same time, although for Fontane a relatively dark work and decidedly not a typical novel of manners and witty dialogue, *Mathilde Möhring* is by no means bogged down in the painfully accurate rendering of German dialect or the baleful workings of heredity and environment. Missing for long stretches, it is true, is the humorous undertone characteristic of his treatment of those on the lower rungs of the social ladder, not to mention the symbolic substructure that often provides interpretive starting points for many of his tales. Nevertheless, typical Fontane traits are easily discernible. Dialogue as well as internal monologue remain a primary technique of characterization. Above all, satirical irony permeates the whole of this, one of Fontane's most ambiguous works.

This is particularly evident in regard to the title character. Compared with other Fontane heroines, *Mathilde Möhring* comes off poorly indeed. The master portrayer of feminine charm leaves his petit bourgeois Mathilde with next to none. Variously described as gaunt, with grayish complexion, watery blue eyes, and stringy ash-blonde hair, the calculating Mathilde is redeemed by no graces or ennobling personality traits. None of the endearing qualities of other Fontane heroines like Lene or Effi betray any sign of the author's affection for this character. Apart from prudence, industriousness, pluck, and practicality, only her ironically stressed "cameo-profile," a backward compliment at best, implying a personality bereft of feminine warmth, speaks for her. Reuter (Reuter, 697) justly characterizes her as the most masculine of Fontane's heroines, and there is no question that throughout much of the story she keeps her femininity well under wraps, doling it out to the ardent Hugo only in small portions.

Mathilde Möhring is unquestionably Fontane's most biting satire both of that uniquely Prussian quality of unremitting self-advancement known as *Streberei* and of the middle-class drive for respectability. Thus the lodestar of the heroine's life has been her father's last words, "Mathilde, stay respectable" (HF I/4, 577). Accordingly, she has stringent standards. Besides moral respectability, it is her social image that preoccupies Mathilde. Frau Runtschen, whom the Möhrings for reasons of status employ as a cleaning woman, is for her not only the representative of an impoverishment to be avoided but of everything she considers low-class. Thus, in Hugo's rejection of the old woman on aesthetic grounds, she perceives confirmation that he possesses a potential she can shape to her own ends. At the same time, while snobbishly rejecting honest poverty for its ugliness, she also repudiates the vulgar tastelessness of the parvenu Schultze as equally beneath contempt. Countering her in the quest for status is her mother, who timidly fears any risks that might imperil their present threadbare respectability. Symptomatic is their dispute over whether a newly acquired chaise longue is to be ostentatiously sat upon or left chastely unused. For Mathilde, who argues, "you shouldn't make yourself too small, then people just keep on making you smaller" (HF I/4/ 626), there is no question but that it is only through the display of wealth that the respect she values will come.

In her calculating devotion to her goal, Mathilde is a sister to Jenny Treibel. Moreover, what she sets out to do—to hitch her wagon to Hugo's star—is no worse than Corinna Schmidt's original intention. Yet we cannot forget that Corinna ultimately repudiates this path as an junworthy step to the gross materialism represented by Jenny. Making Mathilde's single-minded pursuit of advancement even more obnoxious is the smug confidence with which she carries out her program. Time and again she asserts that her plans will turn out as she expects and rejects her mother's anxious warnings that although she may calculate everything in advance, she can also miscalculate (HF I/4, 606).

Yet it is at this point that the character of Mathilde becomes ambiguously problematic. Almost as though Fontane had a love-hate relationship with her and what she represents as a woman, as is suggested by the diverse interpretations of her character, an argument can be made that much in her is also worthy of respect. She is opportunistic, but, given her circumstances, who can complain when she takes advantage of what life sends her way? Moreover, unflagging filial devotion marks her relationship to her whining and timid mother, and the resolute forthrightness with which she goes about her campaign is not unworthy of admiration. There is nothing hypocritical about her, nor does a false or ostentatious sentimentality render her, like Jenny Treibel, an object of ridicule. She never hides her intentions and only once (in the matter of the *Landrat* [county governor]) does she resort to what might be regarded as duplicity. Her self-confidence, although trying, as well as her deft, almost behaviorist manipulation of the otherwise diffident and unfocused Hugo Großmann, are also not undeserving of a certain respect.

True, Mathilde has no real antagonist in Hugo, who in his flabby self-indulgence is a weakling closely related to the pantywaist Leopold Treibel. Through interior monologue and discussion with his friend Rybinski, another variant of the déclassé nobleman-actor later to be found in *Die Poggenpuhls* (*The Poggepuhl Family*), as well as his vague desire to live as a lion tamer, Hugo's character achieves a certain comic-pathetic dimension, especially when it is evident that it is he who is tamed. Through the leitmotiv of his recollections of Rybinski's unencumbered existence as actor and swain, he is one of Fontane's best characterizations of the weak hero, and in his incongruent devotion to Schiller and the unfettered world of the circus, a hapless dilettante not unworthy of the early Thomas Mann.

But is Mathilde to be understood as representative? Gotthard Erler sees her as typical of lower-class figures who seek to make their fortune in a respectable fashion.[32] Werner Hoffmeister (Hoffmeister, 147) also sees her story as part of a typical social process, while Mahal (Mahal, 36), developing a case for an interpretation of Mathilde as a veiled Bismarck figure, holds that she goes her own way totally alone. Müller-Seidel (Müller-Seidel, 328ff.) argues that ambivalence, Fontane's unwillingness to take a stand for either party, Mathilde or Hugo, is in fact the ultimate message of the work.

Yet the preponderance of negative factors suggests satire and caricature as the ultimate intent of the work. Given the realities of the age, situations similar to Mathilde's were undoubtedly common. *Frau Jenny Treibel* represents an obvious parallel, and feminine domination in ascending the social ladder is almost archetypical. Moreover, if we look closely enough, a certain parallel figure can by found in the story itself in none other than Möhring's landlord, Schultze.

Fontane's scorn for the self-satisfied little man lies just below the surface. Schultze is an example of the quick rise to position and wealth of many in the early speculative years of the Reich. But in her own way Mathilde too is a speculator—not with money, of course, but with the only capital she has at hand, her feminine guile, which she invests in the best opportunity that fate makes available.[33] Thus in her relentless striving, she is the petit-bourgeois personification of the self-serving materialism, provincial narrowness, tastelessness, lack of charm and breadth combined with arrogance that Fontane reluctantly found in the values of the new Reich.

Nothing underscores this more than the outcome of her efforts. Her plans do ultimately miscarry, as her mother has warned, because in her supreme self-confidence Mathilde has miscalculated. The handsome Hugo, whose full beard and impressive looks she has counted on, proves not only a weakling in matters of character but physically as well. His first sickness, a children's malaise, makes this clear from the outset. Thus it is a harsh irony that precisely at the moment when Mathilde has gained her sought-after title and is able to hobnob with blue bloods and can reckon herself to "die obren Zehntausend" ("the upper ten thousand") (HF I/4, 656), and, to top it all off, is at last even ready to permit her long-repressed femininity to express itself by allowing Frau Schmädicke's bedroom lamp—now garishly improved with ruby-colored glass—to fulfill its erotic mission, that Hugo is laid low. It cannot escape the reader that the supremely confident young woman has been given a comeuppance that puts her back where she started. Is it poetic justice for overweening petit-bourgeois ambition? Or is her story another example of Robert Burns's apostrophe regarding the best-laid plans of mice and men?

The old skeptic Fontane gives us no clear answer, although the weight of the evidence suggests poetic justice. Instead, with characteristic ambiguity, he presents in the last chapters a rehabilitated Mathilde, who with Prussian pluck and fortitude picks up the pieces of her life. Caring for her mother, and with the prestige she has gained in her new career as a teacher, she holds her own. Mellowed by her contact with Hugo, she is now even concerned for the impoverished Frau Runtschen, and goes so far as to regret that she has no pledge of Hugo's love, as she ostentatiously refers to the unconceived child, for her mother to rock. But barrenness is the ultimate meaning of Mathilde's striving, and Fontane also allowed himself a final irony to underscore it. After briefly mentioning the memorial wreaths laid twice a year at the grave of her hopes, the last sentence (clumsily deleted by Ettlinger) laconically reports the marriage of Rebecca Silberstein. The Jewish girl whom Mathilde found "pretty" but not particularly useful in her plan to put the town on the map has obviously received the ruby-glassed lamp promised her and in Woldenstein, where fate has denied Mathilde her victory, will fulfill her womanly destiny in maternal affluence, while Mathilde Möhring's life in Berlin has scarcely been changed.

The Masterpiece: *Effi Briest*

A product of the period from late 1888 through the spring of 1894, Fontane's unchallenged masterwork, *Effi Briest,* was serialized in the *Deutsche Rundschau* from October 1894 through March of 1895. Three editions followed in the same year under the imprint of F. Fontane Co., although they were dated 1896. With grim satisfaction, the author could justifiably look upon this novel, published in his seventy-sixth year, as his "first real success." Despite reliance on a few well-worn conventions, such as accidentally discovered love letters, and a relatively sentimentalized ending,[34] there can be no question but that stylistically, thematically, and artistically, *Effi Briest* represents the pinnacle of Fontane's fiction, the finest social novel in German letters between Goethe's *Die Wahlverwandschaften* (1808) and Thomas Mann's *Buddenbrooks* (1901), published only two years after Fontane's death.

Fontane himself seemed astonished at the ease with which the story took shape. With a metaphor he invoked several times to account for his creative process, he described the first draft as having been written as if with a psychograph, an instrument employed by spiritualists to record utterances of the dead (HF I/4, 706). Aware that it was his finest work to date, he was so painstaking with his revisions he became seriously ill. On his physician's advice, he temporarily abandoned the project in favor of writing his memoirs, *Meine Kinderjahre* (My childhood years) (1893), as therapy in order to regain his strength to complete the novel.

Effi Briest is the story of a girl from the Prussian aristocracy who at age 17 is married for reasons of class and family ambition to Geerd von Innstetten, a former suitor of her mother's more than twice her age. Immaturity, temperament, impressionability, boredom, anxiety, and alienation lead her into an affair. Several years later, after she has successfully grown into the role of a model Wilhelmine wife and mother, her now-forgotten involvement is discovered by her husband. Holding to the ossified aristocratic code of honor, he challenges and kills her former lover, knowing it will destroy Effi and his own life as well. Divorced, ostracized, alienated from her child, rejected even by her parents, and abandoned by all but a faithful servant girl and a dog, Effi is broken in spirit and health. Too late she is permitted to return home to the parental estate, where she dies.

Dinner gossip with a publisher's wife provided Fontane with the details surrounding the divorce of Armand Léon Baron von Ardenne from his wife Elizabeth (Else), whose story formed the nucleus of *Effi Briest*.[35] Else von Plotho had married Ardenne, older by five years and an officer in the famous Zieten Hussars, in 1873. In Düsseldorf a liaison between the district judge (*Amtsrichter*) Hartwich and Else von Ardenne developed that survived Ardenne's transfer to Berlin, and the lovers laid plans to divorce their respective spouses and marry. Discovering their letters, however, the aggrieved husband challenged and mortally wounded his rival in a duel in the fall of 1886. A divorce was granted in April 1887. Imprisoned for dueling, Ardenne was nevertheless pardoned by Wilhelm I and continued his army career, retiring as a lieutenant general in 1904 after a dispute with Wilhelm II and continuing to write military history until his death in 1919. His former wife, who thereafter devoted herself to charitable work, died at the age of 99 in 1952, long after the world in which a tragedy such as hers could take place had ceased to exist.

Effi Briest is one of Fontane's most graceful compositional achievements. Its 36 chapters steeped in an autumnal mood and four narrative blocks associated with different locations and psychological states attest to the author's formal mastery. Effi's life is recounted from just moments before her misfortune starts with her betrothal to Innstetten to its ultimate consequence, her death. Further contributing to a sense of symmetry, beginning and ending take place in the paradisiacal shelter of Hohen-Cremmen, the Briest family estate. Middle sections are located at opposite poles of bureaucratic activity in the Second Reich— an isolated and closely knit provincial town, modeled after the seacoast community of Swinemünde in which the author had spent part of his boyhood, and the imperial capital. These segments are themselves roughly divided by turning points in Effi's life, the arrival of her seducer, Major von Crampas, and his death at the hand of her husband.

A masterpiece of German realist fiction, depicting with copious detail life among the privileged in the Second Empire, while implicitly critical of the petrified mores of the Prussian aristocracy, *Effi Briest* is another of Fontane's novels interwoven with a complex web of ambiguities, symbols, and leitmotivs. Fontane always subscribed to the view that it was the artist's obligation to render a higher reality than that of everyday existence. It was a conviction that kept him head and shoulders above most of his younger naturalist contemporaries for whom literature had become a relentless duplication of the implacable effects of heredity and environment on the individual in a world devoid of beauty. Thus it was not merely the tawdry details of the Ardenne affair that set the writer's creative processes in motion. Rather, the pregnant call "Else, komm," part of the original story as he had heard it from his informant, was one of the chief factors igniting his interest. "The appearance of the girls at the windows overgrown with wine leaves," he maintained, "the redheads, the call and then their ducking down and disappearing, made *such* an impression on me, that from *this* scene the whole long story evolved."[36]

The author's emphasis on this instant underscores the spiritual subsoil of the work, in which predestination, realistic psychology, and mythology intermingle. With the call "Effi, komm," at the end of the second chapter, mythopoetic forces are brought into play. As we have seen, Fontane had a tendency to classify personalities and was fascinated by feminine types drawn from myth and fairy tale. Above all, Melusine, the mysterious water nixie who vainly desires to be a real woman and participate in human love and suffering, fascinated him. To the figure of Effi Briest a host of such mythical qualities have been imparted. Along with traits of Melusine, for instance, she may be seen as a negative Cinderella,[37] a penitent Magdalene, and even a replication of the Pre-Raphaelite conception of Mary in a modern context.[38] And, of course, both her husband and Dr. Rummschüttel characterize her as a daughter of Eve (Eva-Effi), the original temptress and penitent.[39] At the same time, her juvenile clothes, the legacy of an English girl the author spotted vacationing in the Harz mountains, her gestures, her boyish enthusiasm, and her naive views on love and marriage all emphatically make clear that although on the threshold of womanhood at the outset of her tragedy, Effi is still an immature, androgynous child of nature. For her the social order she is about to enter has scarcely any meaning beyond misconstrued impressions gained from her mother, who is also not wholly unaware of her daughter's unreadiness for the role thrust upon her.

Once more, Fontane's sense of destiny is the chief structural principle. Effi is predestined to fail. Although eager to emulate her mother, who herself has followed a course similar to the one planned for Effi, she is deterministically portrayed as being far closer in personality to her father, who makes no pretense about his preference for an unencumbered existence on his Brandenburg estate, where "every green leaf and the wild wine leaves" (HF I/4, 21) offer him pleasure. Effi too is happiest in the idyllic freedom of Hohen-Cremmen with its heliotropes, pond, and plane trees. Her character, from the outset unstable and impressionable, is ill-prepared for the boredom she encounters in marriage and for the insensitivity of her husband. As has been frequently pointed out, her tendency to court danger in the belief that somehow she will escape harm, symbolically represented in her love of swinging, is one of the primary elements leading to her fall.[40] Yet, despite her natural tendencies, in keeping with the demands imposed by her birth, rank, and sex, she is compelled to turn from the world of freedom, which portentously calls her back at the outset of the novel, to the realm of rigidly circumscribed functions, public as well as private, that constituted a woman's place in the upper levels of Wilhelmine society.

Thus the immature and naive girl is forced not only to become a wife, head of household, and mother; she must also assume the representational obligations incumbent upon her as the Baroness von Innstetten, wife of the district commissioner, roles for which, despite her eagerness to measure up, she is scarcely fit. The unwillingness of those closest to her to face the incompatibility of Effi's personality with the unbending societal structure that ultimately destroys her is, of course, the ultimate meaning of the ambiguous leitmotiv associated with her easygoing father, "That's far too big a subject." (HF I/4, 296).

Another aspect of Briest's leitmotiv is contained in the broader social ramifications of the novel. Through a complex of motifs, Fontane underscores that his heroine is a victim in a peculiarly Teutonic rite. Scarcely has her story begun than Effi's destiny is foreshadowed in the ritual she and her playmates create as they sink berry skins, left by her reddish-blonde friend with the particularly Germanic name Hertha, into the pond. The act reminds Effi of "poor, unfortunate women" who are drowned, "naturally because of unfaithfulness." To Hertha's response that such things do not occur "here," Effi laughingly replies, "No, not here, . . . things like that don't happen here. But in Constantinople . . ." (HF I/4, 14).

What follows, of course, clearly refutes the girl's belief that such ceremonies occur only in exotic climes. Prussia is shown to be barbaric in its own fashion, a place where fallen women are punished in a far more subtle manner than by drowning. It is one of the ambiguities of this richly ambiguous work that the words of her playmate Hertha, *"Effi, komm"* (HF I/4, 18), with which her story begins (and ends, when she is called home with the same phrase), may be interpreted either as a call to return to childhood or as a summons to participate in the sacrificial ritual the author postulates as her life. This motif is further elaborated when in the summer after her adultery Effi comes across sacrificial stones dedicated to the Germanic mother-goddess Hertha and, horrified by connotations of blood sacrifice, flees. Near the conclusion of the novel the significance of these episodes becomes clear. Recollecting Lake Hertha, Effi declares an aversion for the Wendish tribes she associates with its rituals. Choirmaster Jahnke, father of the playmate whose call initiates her sacrificial path, corrects Effi's faulty knowledge of German prehistory. "But you see, those weren't Wends," he tells her. "That whole business about sacrificial stones and Lake Hertha, that was much much earlier, . . . pure Teutons, from whom we're all descended."

Effi's response, "Of course, from whom we're all descended, the Jahnkes for sure and perhaps the Briests as well" (HF I/4, 280), suggests that at last she is becoming aware of the role thrust upon her, for it has long since become evident that in giving Effi as a child bride for reasons of caste and social advancement, her parents have delivered up their daughter to a rite every bit as barbaric as those dedicated to the Teutonic Earth Mother. Another aspect of the same concept in a rhetorical matrix is the outburst of Wüllersdorf, Innstetten's second, as they discuss the impending duel the latter feels compelled to fight: "This cult of honor of ours is idolatry, but we've got to subjugate ourselves to it, as long as the idol goes on" (HF I/4, 237).

Geert von Innstetten, through whom the rites associated with Effi's fate are carried out, is the most thorough study of traits regarded as typically Prussian in Fontane's oeuvre. The gap in age between husband and wife is obviously a determining factor in the breakdown of their relationship. Yet dividing them above all is Innstetten's almost stereotypically Prussian masculine personality, rigorously correct, coolly objective, efficient, and emotionally repressed. At the moment of crisis, even though paradoxically he no longer really believes in it, it is the code of honor, rather than love, compassion, and forgiveness, upon which he relies. Thus, aside from being arguably his most subtle work, *Effi Briest* is undoubtedly Fontane's sharpest fictional attack on the inflexible ethos underlying the Prussian aristocracy in the late nineteenth century, a caste shown as incapable "of escaping the prison of a role determined not by the requirements of human nature, but by an empty social and ethical code" (Thum, 115).

Effi Briest is thus like *Schach von Wuthenow,* with which it is obviously related, a uniquely Prussian book, a story that could happen only where the governing ethos is that of the military camp into which the Prussian state had been turned over the centuries by the Hohenzollerns and their adherents. The discussions between Innstetten and Wüllersdorf both before and after the duel with Crampas expose the decrepitude and inhumanity of the aristocratic code. The code of the duel, essentially an offshoot of the militarism infusing Prussian society since the days of the Soldier King, Friedrich Wilhelm I, and officially forbidden by royal decree and under attack in the Reichstag even as the novel was being written, was nevertheless still very much alive in Prussia in the declining years of the nineteenth century. As a caste straitjacket and metaphor for the petrification of the aristocratic ethos, it had been touched upon earlier by Fontane in *Cécile* and *Irrungen,*

Wirrungen. In the latter, Botho von Rienäcker contemplates the monument to a slain nobleman, the former Berlin police chief von Hinckeldey, who, despite the legal prohibition of dueling he was sworn to uphold, has nevertheless gone to his death on the so-called field of honor for no other reason than what Botho characterizes as "a preconception of the nobility, a class whim, more powerful even than reason" (HF I/2, 405).

Gallons of ink have been spilled on the motif of the Chinaman's ghost with which Effi becomes obsessed during her stay in Kessin. Its role has been questioned since the novel's appearance. Fontane, however, had no doubts. To the Swiss critic Joseph Viktor Widman on 19 November 1895, he asserted that he found the motif "interesting in and of itself." It was, he continued, "a pivot point [Drehpunkt] of the entire story" and an element not included "just for the fun of it" (HF I/4, 706). Whether it can be considered a symbol of Effi's angst, or as part of the complex of elements associated with Oriental sacrifice, or whether it represents Effi's half-unconscious inclination to violate the principle of order inherent in Bismarckian society,[41] or is simply to be relegated to the dustbin of bric-a-brac left over from German Poetic Realism[42] is an open question. A figment of Effi's impressionable imagination, its primary function is unquestionably as part of the psychological matrix of the story. Fontane leaves it as another of the novel's ambiguities whether Innstettin actually employs her fear of the ghost to control Effi, as Crampas, for reasons of his own, suggests. Once it has been suggested, however, to the impressionable young woman that her husband is manipulating her, it intensifies Effi's alienation and powerfully contributes to the state of mind that allows her to wander from the straight and narrow path suggested in the title of the play directed by Crampas, in which in more than one way she plays the leading role.

The sentiment surrounding Effi's death is a typical closure for the tragic heroine-victim. Not the least of the work's ironies is the fact that in the dialectic of her nature, the child-woman scarcely penetrates to the reality of her role as a victim. In her last scene she confesses her rage against her former husband, yet relates how under the ameliorating influence of illness and the spiritual healing of Hohen-Cremmen, she is able to find his actions justifiable. Conciliation and transfiguring acceptance are indeed part of the operatic ethos of the nineteenth-century tradition, and richly at home in Wilhelmine art. Child of his age that he was, Fontane accepted such conciliatory transfiguration as a basic tenet of his own philosophy, although, it must be admitted, he rarely applied it with so thick a brush as in the closing pages of *Effi Briest*.

But Fontane's saving skepticism also mitigates the sentimental tone of the final pages. Not only are we left with the bitter irony of Briest's ambiguous "Das ist ein *zu* weites Feld" (HF I/4, 296), but as the reader clearly knows, Effi's insight is relative; Innstetten himself no longer shares her view; he has long since come to the conclusion that his act and remaining life have been meaningless (HF I/4, 289). Effi's remarks, underscoring the pathos of her situation, can be taken as a final authorial flourish with which to bid farewell to an endearing heroine. At the same time, however, her last statement regarding her husband, that "he had a great deal that was good in his nature and was as noble as someone can be who is without real love" (HF I/4, 294), may be taken at face value; it is an indictment not only of Innstetten but of the entire society he represents, a society in which formalities, appearances, and mummified rituals have displaced kindness, forgiveness, and love.

Chapter Five
Beyond the Reich

Fontane did not wish to be viewed merely as a writer of Berlin novels and several times chose topics that would prevent his being categorized as such. Yet even the novels that are deliberately placed outside Prussia tangentially touch upon aspects of the Prussian character, as we shall see. Moreover, there is no question, given the writer's social and political concern for his homeland and the nature of his talent, which rested in large part on empirical observation, that his strength lay in portrayal of what he knew best. Of the three works that take place beyond the Reich, only *Unwiederbringlich,* which is set in Schleswig and Denmark, areas close to the author's homeland with which he felt a spiritual kinship, has received substantial critical acclaim. *Graf Petöfy* with an Austro-Hungarian atmosphere, and *Quitt* (Paid in full), which takes place in part in America, and which because of the fatalistic atmosphere permeating the story will be treated in chapter 6, have generally been relegated to the limbo of nearly forgotten works.

Graf Petöfy

Published in 1884 between *Schach von Wuthenow* and *Unterm Birnbaum* (Beneath the pear tree), *Graf Petöfy* (Count Petöfy) takes up anew a theme explored earlier in *L'Adultera,* the marriage of a younger woman to an older man. The stimulus was a newspaper notice of the wedding in May 1880 between the actress Johanna Buska, whom Fontane had admired for some years on the Berlin stage, and Hungarian Count Nikolaus Casimir Török von Szendrö, 68, a major general in the Austrian army.

Fontane worked on the novel from January 1881 until autumn 1883, and the story first appeared in the *Deutsche Roman Bibliothek zu Über Land und Meer* (German novel supplement to Across land and sea), between July and August 1884. In June 1884, only weeks before its appearance, Count Török's death was announced. Vacationing in the Harz mountains, Fontane cut out the notice and sent it to his wife with the ironic comment, "Török is Petöfy and Buska is Franziska—but she will probably be less creative and marry some Egon or other for sure" (HF, I/1, 1001). This prophecy was quickly fulfilled when the lady in question married the director of the German Theater in Prague later the same year.

Nearly 70, the title character of Fontane's version of the story, the Viennese-Hungarian Count Adam Petöfy, is taken by the charming young actress Franziska Franz. Renowned for her ingénue and soubrette roles, Franziska, a pastor's daughter from Prussia's Baltic provinces, proves a serious and down-to-earth young woman who despite her stage successes yearns for a life of security and peace. Learning of his intent to marry Franziska, Countess Judith, whose devotion to Catholicism matches Petöfky's worldliness, warns her brother regarding differences in age, class, and religion. Nevertheless the count sues for the young woman's hand and she accepts. Earnestly she attempts to fulfill her new role as mistress of the Petöfy estate in Hungary, but, shunned by the local nobility and not at home in the strange Magyar world, she grows bored and lonely. A visit by Countess Judith and her nephew Egon, to whom Franziska has always felt drawn, proves fateful. Recognizing that he has placed Franziska in an impossible position, the count ends his life. Franziska, however, chooses not to marry Egon but instead to carry on as Countess Petöfy by devoting herself to the estates and embracing Catholicism.

Again the point of departure was psychological. At the same time, much about *Graf Petöfy* reflects the conventional novel of high society. The milieu is that of the salons and personal apartments of the upper class of Vienna and a nearby spa. Drawing room conversations, homeward strolls, breakfast discussions, summer outings, situations well known to the Fontane reader from *Schach von Wuthenow* and *L'Adultera*, make up the general itinerary. Yet there are innovations. The primary thrust of the novel is not conflict between the individual and the social order but the personal quest for a meaningful life. In the more exotic second part, in which the spiritual conflict emanating from earlier events is carried through, the theme of the mystical hold of Catholicism, touched upon in *Schach,* is returned to and the author relies heavily on the symbolic connotations of the landscape to focus on the inner being of the new Countess Petöfy.

Thus, despite the title, the central figure is actually Franziska. The significant social exchanges of the first half of the novel demonstrate her winning conversational gifts. Franziska's romantic impressions of

Petöfy's native Hungary and, later, recollections of her Baltic home—drawn from Fontane's lifelong affinity for the Hungarian poet Lenau and his childhood memories of Swinemünde—captivate the count. At the same time, conversations with Egon and her maidservant Hannah reveal the private side of the young woman's character, suggesting her incipient feelings for the count's nephew and her yearning for a more fulfilling existence, which she hopes ultimately to satisfy in marriage to the elderly aristocrat.

Three chapters (10–12), each presented from a differing personal perspective, give the arguments for and against the marriage. The elderly suitor expects only that Franziska will enliven his declining years through her vivacious conversation. For his part, he offers a "relationship . . . built on perfect freedom, a marital pact that instead of the usual qualifying paragraphs has a single white page. Carte blanche," limited only by "discretion. . . , decorum, dehors" (HF I/1, 751).

Believing herself immune to passion, Franziska feels that she can meet such conditions. Although she is concerned about having to sublimate herself to the needs and personality of the count, her ambition and confidence mistakenly lead her to believe that the duties incumbent upon her as Countess Petöfy are merely another role that life has offered her. "After all," she tells her maid, Hannah, "what is it that matters in the so-called upper sphere anyway? Simply just being able to wear a train and put on or take off a glove with a certain amount of style. . . . So much in life is nothing but play-acting anyway, and whoever is familiar from a professional standpoint with this game and all its ins and outs in advance is already a step ahead of the others and can easily transfer it from the stage into real life" (HF I/1, 759).

In the second section of the novel, a dark atmosphere rarely evoked by Fontane prevails. Various elements such as a brooding Madonna suggest spiritual longing and the mystical qualities of Catholicism. Contrary to his usual wont, Fontane indulges in a good deal of landscape description.[1] A mountainous landscape with stream and freshet as well as nearby Lake Arpa, rich in ominous suggestions of repressed passion, dominate the atmosphere as Franziska finds the role she has undertaken more challenging than anticipated. The symbolic brush is applied heavily here, especially in a scene describing the outbreak of suppressed feelings between Egon and Franziska as they are caught in a whirlpool crossing the lake after an expedition to find a lost child.

Notwithstanding its seeming conventionality as a novel of high society in an Austro-Hungarian setting, *Graf Petöfy* also offers a study in

Prussian character. Although Fontane endows his heroine with the self-assured and sophisticated gifts of conversation and wit, he also makes her a woman of a severe Prussian Lutheran background. Beyond what she interprets as her thoughtful and even calculating Prussian sobriety (HF I/1, 698), a portion of north European romantic yearning is also part of her nature. It is she who interprets an aspect of her personality as "a longing for the more simple, the more natural things" (HF I/1, 697). It is traits such as these that are intended to make her acceptance of Petöfy's strange offer comprehensible; they also raise the novel a notch above the conventional belles lettres category to which critics have occasionally condemned it.[2]

In Franziska's search for religious security, the agnostic-Calvinist Fontane deepens what would otherwise be merely a conventional novel set among the social elite. Fontane's fascination with the religious question, stimulated in exchanges with his Catholic friends the Wagenheims, is evident in a number of his works. Numerous religious individuals as well as the ineffectual representatives of the clergy who people his works are testimony to his conviction that traditional Protestantism did not always fulfill an inborn mystical yearning. Count Adam, himself an agnostic, expresses the need to Franziska:

When you get right down to it, our weak nature is really stronger than our strongest lack of faith, which at the bottom is just braggadocio and hasn't got a bit of courage. I know that from myself. And as soon as anything is really at stake or maybe just a bit of gout or a twinge puts in an appearance, I sneak a look over at my Saint Stephen there, standing over my desk, just like that Madonna over yours, and I say, "Now get to work there, Stephanerl, and do your bit for a Magyar and honest Christian fellow." And you know, Fränzl, it seems to me, something like that is hiding in every one of us, and in the last analysis, even in a sweet little heretic's soul as well. (HF I/1, 767)

Discussions between the countess and the Redemptorist priest, Pater Feßler, allow the author not only to foreshadow Franziska's path from Protestantism to Catholicism but also to characterize Prussians from a conservative Austrian-Catholic point of view. Feßler's discourses on religion and culture, his dissertations on the Prussian national character, serve to explain Franziska's decision to consecrate herself as the widowed Countess Petöfy to seeking fulfillment not in marriage but in spiritual sublimation. The primary symbol of the work is clarified in this context by Feßler, who, recognizing Franziska's inner strength, asserts that "the young lady's soul is of an alloy from which a bell can emerge that will ring true" (HF I/1, 740).

Variations on the bell motif throw light on a characteristic of a number of Fontane's novels—the dominant symbol and its elaboration. In this case, the initial form occurs in Franziska's childhood recollection of ringing the call to evening prayer (HF I/1, 708). That the bell rope was pulled from her hands suggests that perhaps the Protestant bell had not been the right one for her. The interweaving of her destiny with bells is also evidenced by their portentous sounding at significant stations on her journey toward personal fulfillment. A bell marks the arrival of a bouquet from Egon as she rationalizes her decision to marry the count (HF I/1, 761). Similarly, another announces the approaching steamer that brings the letter revealing Egon's arrival at Schloß Arpa (HF I/1, 812). Most portentiously, when she arrives for the first time at Castle Arpa, the bell cracks (HF I/1, 764), an event she interprets as a bad omen. By the end, however, the reader realizes that its cracking applies not to her but to the count. Another allusion to the bell rope and Franziska's path to her ultimate destiny occurs when a pigeon is discovered building its nest in the bell tower with a long strand of yarn, immediately before the arrival of Count Egon (HF I/1, 818). The fulfillment of Feßler's prophecy is achieved in the last chapter in which two bells, representing the two Countesses Petöfy, united in charitable commitment through Catholicism, resound over the Petöfy estates (HF I/1, 864).

Modern criticism has not been kind to *Graf Petöfy*. In 1919, Wandrey relegated it to the realm of secondary works, praiseworthy at best for its cultured style, but utterly lacking in convincing ethnic background. Presaging critics such as Demetz and Martini, he condemned it as "throughout on the level of the commonplace trivial novel" (Wandrey, 313). Demetz, for whom the entire ouevre between *Schach von Wuthenow* (1883) and *Irrungen, Wirrungen* (1888) lies in the "depths of commonplace belles lettres," argued that *Graf Petöfy* as well as *Cécile* "entrust themselves to the inherited but lifeless methodology of the novel of society, without tightening it by bold insight or artistic energy" (Demetz, 164–65).

In the light of the masterworks that followed, *Graf Petöfy* is indeed inferior. Even Franziska's spiritual quest cannot alter the fact that, as with *Cécile,* it fails to take the social realities of nineteenth-century Europe into account and treats the aristocracy and its ways as a lifestyle whose survival is a given, at a time when the author saw both becoming historically irrelevant. This being said, however, *Graf Petöfy* cannot be ignored. In its pages Fontane demonstrates a new level of mastery of the novel of high society and of the techniques used in the works that follow. It occupies itself with a circle of themes that continually fascinated the author—theater and life, the spiritual pull of religion and the mystique of Catholicism, as well as the dialectic of North and South and the art of conversation itself, that *causerie* which was Fontane's stock in trade. Underrated because of the more successful—and historically relevant—novels that followed, it nevertheless deserves a closer look.

Unwiederbringlich

As reported to the editor of the prestigious *Deutsche Rundschau*, which first published it in 1891, Fontane's source for *Unwiederbringlich* was a letter received from a friend in February 1885 describing events at the court of Strelitz in the Baltic principality of Mecklenburg. According to this, a north German nobleman, later identified as Baron Karl Hans Friedrich von Mahlzahn,[3] serving there as a retainer, succumbed to the charms of a lady-in-waiting and precipitately demanded a divorce from his wife. Having done so, he encountered only amused scorn from the object of his infatuation and was forced to recognize that he had played the fool. After two years abroad, a reconciliation with his former wife led to their remarrying. Shortly thereafter, the baroness was found dead, leaving in her room nothing but a note bearing the word *unwiederbringlich* (irretrievable, beyond recall). Wolfgang Paulsen has pointed out that parallels also exist between the work and the marital vicissitudes of Fontane's close friend Bernhard von Lepel, not to mention Fontane's own crisis-ridden marriage.[4] Work on the novel, begun in 1887, competed with a multitude of other projects so that not until December 1890 was the final draft complete. A book edition, dated 1892, was published by Wilhelm Herz in November 1891.

Discretion as well as artistic considerations led Fontane to alter the locale of his story to Denmark and Schleswig in the late 1850s. The disposition of the duchies of Schleswig and Holstein, their integration into Denmark or existence as German states, was at the time a burning issue and later became one of the milestones passed on Prussia's march to a unified Germany. Just as he had employed the Wagner debate in *L'Adultera*, Fontane made use of this former political controversy in the novel's psychological substructure to underscore the antagonism between his principal characters.[5] The plot, however, generally follows the original source. Count Helmuth Holk von Holkenäs, married for many years to his severe but loving wife Christine, is called to attendance at the court of Princess Marie Eleonore in Copenhagen. There, after first being struck by the charms of the lovely widow Hansen, he succumbs to the spell of the coquettish Ebba Rosenberg, a lady-in-waiting. Without discussing his plans with Ebba, he hurries home to demand a divorce. Deeply hurt, his wife refuses to reason with him. Returning to Copenhagen, Holk discovers that Ebba does not consider him a serious suitor. After some time in London, he returns to his homeland. A reconciliation is arranged and Christine and Holk remarry. Christine, however, is unable to forget the past, and shortly after their marriage she drowns herself in the sea.

As Demetz (Demetz, 166) has pointed out, the novel is divided into four narrative blocks, each dominated by its feminine figures. To Christine fall chapters 1 through 9. Roughly the first half of the middle between chapters 10 and 18 are devoted to Holk's vacillation between the physical charms of Brigitte Hansen and the provocative Ebba. Chapters 19 to 30 narrate the excursion with Ebba to Castle Fredericksborg, culminating in adultery, conflagration, and confrontation. The last four chapters are given over to the return of Holk to Christine and Holkenäs and the mournful outcome of the attempt to restore what has been lost forever. As noted by Fontane, locations also dominate,[6] with the first part devoted to Holkenäs, the second to Copenhagen, the third to Fredericksborg, and the fourth again to Holkenäs. There an upper-bourgeois idyll prevails, in which the provincial nobility are depicted as country landowners. Life is comfortably uncomplicated, and the simple pleasures, a close relationship with the local clergy, discussions of cattle, whist, reading, a conversation on the beach, a song after dinner, in short, the mundane activities of comfortable country folk, regulate daily life. In Copenhagen, by contrast, gossip and political intrigue are the order of the day. In an almost rococo world where court ceremony and an eighteenth-century attitude of lax sophistication and innuendo hold sway, Holk soon finds himself hopelessly out of his element.

Characterization reveals Fontane at the height of his powers. Rejecting "the modern idol of nationalism" (HF I/2, 583), Christine nevertheless reveals herself as an adherent of a German rather than a Danish Schleswig, although at the time, 1859 to 1861, Danish dominion still prevailed. As a Christian, she finds Prussian militarism abhorrent and rejects its domination of her homeland, yet her devotion to duty as well as the Lutheran confession betray an inherent affinity for Prussian values. Thus her fundamentalism and desire for "Gothic, angels and palms" (HF I/2, 579) in the style of Peter Cornelius reflect the pietistic renewal that flourished under the patronage of Friedrich Wilhelm IV, explaining her sympathetic interest in the condition of that ill-fated Prussian monarch.[7]

Just as he does not share his wife's spiritual fervor, Holk also differs from her politically. He holds to the party of Schleswig-Holsteiners loyal to the Danish monarchy. As thoughtless in political matters as in moral strictness, he refuses to recognize Prussia's threat to Denmark in northern Europe and repudiates its historical role and future possibilities. It is an irony, then, that once in Copenhagen, the Danish courtier is looked upon more as a German than a Dane and even as an adherent of the Prussian cause. His underestimation of Prussia's future and devotion to the moribund Danish cause obviously expose him to the informed reader as a dubious judge both of politics and, by inference, of persons, as his involvement with Ebba soon confirms.

It is not merely political differences that contribute to the novel's psychological verisimilitude. The spiritual incompatibility of the pair, suggested, for example, by Christine's desire for a neo-Gothic mausoleum at the same time her husband is planning hygienic new cattle stalls, sets the stage for their differences. That Christine's religiosity and the earnestness with which she pursues it are obsessive[8] is pointed out to her and the reader, who has probably come to a similar conclusion, by her brother. Recalling Goethe's Mittler in *Elective Affinities*, the latter attempts to mediate between husband and wife and, with a genuine Fontanean attitude of avoiding extremes even in a good cause, warns his sister that "It's not the standpoint, it's the *way* one represents it. And there I've got to tell you, you're carrying things too far, it's too much of a good thing" (HF I/2, 619).

Intertwined with unyielding dogmatism and the sternness with which she upholds it are Christine's melancholia and sensitivity. Her depressive personality is quick to see the pessimistic side of every situation. To Holk's exclamation that their castle on the sea will be a joy for them both, she rejoins, "When one is happy, one should not want to be even more happy" (HF I/2, 569), and further dampens his enthusiasm by citing the gloomy final stanza of Uhland's ballad "Das Schloß am Meer" (The castle by the sea), with which Holk ostentatiously describes their new home. Neurotic hypersensitivity characterizes her reaction to the sentimental morbidity of "Der Kirchof" (The Churchyard), a poem by the little-known romantic Wilhelm Waiblinger, innocently rendered as a parlor song by her daughter and a friend. Its final lines—"Pity those, we ought, who hate,/Still more, almost, who love"—become a motto for her life and, ultimately, her death.

No less destructive is Holk's blithe superficiality and impressibility. With good reason, his brother-in-law characterizes him as a "spur of the moment person" *(Augenblicksmensch)* (HF I/2, 595). Yet even his easygoing ways cannot subdue his growing irritation with his wife's persistant earnestness and what he begins to perceive as her supercilious nagging. "I can't succeed in putting you into a friendly mood and tearing you away from your eternal brooding and always taking things so seriously," he tells her in exasperation. "I wonder, is it my fault or yours?" (HF I/2, 607). The call to court removes him from the direct influence of his wife, but does not prevent him from feeling the frustration her letters induce, which is now chronicled in their correspondence. One of the painful ironies and formal touches of the work is that their letters, which in the past were the means of intensifying their love, now become the gauge of their increasing alienation.[9]

Sexuality smolders beneath the surface of *Unwiederbringlich* and not just in the figures of the flirtatious Brigitte Hansen and the cynically hedonistic Ebba. Heide Eilert (Eilert, 542) has argued that "Christine's rigid dogmatism, her displays of superiority, her exaggerated sense of duty" can be viewed as "compensation for withheld emotional gratification, her depressions as self-directed aggressions." In essence, they are a veiled projection of the effect of the repressive Victorian moral code upon women, which, it might be added, is at the bottom of many of Fontane's portrayals of women in marital crisis. Holk too, Eilert notes, can be viewed under a similar lens, inasmuch as the counterpart to female repression in the Victorian scheme is the masculine tendency to separate physical love from spiritual love. Thus as he seeks to justify his adultery, his image of his wife, which, as his brother-in-law suggests, had been progressively determined by her beauty, intelligence, and piety (HF I/2, 595), ultimately yields to frustration at being married to a woman who, by comparison with the warmth and passion he believes he has found in Ebba, he classifies as an iceberg (HF I/2, 772).

Leitmotivs and symbolic elements are once again masterfully integrated into the fabric of the narrative of *Unwiederbringlich*. Fire, a balladesque Nordic-romantic touch, suggests the perils of sexual adventure. As Christine's brother and Pastor Schwarzkoppen discuss

Christine's obsessive piety, a rocket on the horizon turns their conversation to the king's easy ways and the dangers they bode for the realm, a subtle foreshadowing of what is to come. Later, Holk minimizes Ebba's charms by comparing them to "a rocket . . . in the end nothing but pyrotechnics, just artificial" (HF I/2, 698). For her part, the red-headed Ebba delights in teasing her victim with allusions to her nature as an elemental temptress. "In the final analysis," she tells him, "all ballads come down to a bit of Ebba. Ebba is Eve . . . And it's generally known, there's nothing romantic without the apple" (HF I/2, 659).

As Holk's peril increases so does the intensity of the fire imagery. Shortly before his fall, he spends an evening examining—by torchlight—a battle painting of the explosion of the Swedish galleon *Makelos (Unblemished)* in which the admiral perished. Foreshadowed is the approaching destiny of the gallant who only too willingly jeopardizes his unblemished marital fidelity as the fuse of passion lit by Ebba begins to burn. An elaboration occurs in Holk's dream of clinging to a piece of the mast after the catastrophe, drawn by a mermaid Ebba into the deep, to which in a moment of insight on awakening he ironically comments, "She would be capable of something like that" (HF I/2, 716). The high point of the fire imagery is reached in the destruction of Castle Fredericksborg from a blaze begun in an overheated "Ebba-tower," stoked by Ebba's serving girl to warm her own illicit tryst. A final bitter twist is provided by Ebba herself, who curtly signals that the fires of passion are burned out: "Why such a fuss? First it was a bit too hot, then a bit too cold" (HF I/2, 763).

If there is any flaw in *Unwiederbringlich* it is in the expansiveness of the middle chapters. Fontane's penchant for innuendo, witty conversation, and antiquarianism contribute to the atmosphere of boredom and moral laxity at court and to the gradualness of Holk's slide into adultery perhaps, but they may also try the reader's patience. The Hansen episode, craftily inserted by the old master as a preview of the intellectual-sexual firworks Holk encounters in Ebba's justification (HF I/2, 731) of the preferability of amorality to the hypocrisy of virtue, seems in the end too spun out. In similar fashion, a twilight review of stags, reminiscent of the swans of *Schach von Wuthenow,* followed by a lamentation over the disappearance of the poetic and noble (in both senses of the word), adds little to the novel's overall effect, its balladesque poetry notwithstanding.

The last word has yet to be written about the place of this novel in Fontane's oeuvre. Praise for *Unwiederbringlich* has never been lacking. Among the earliest to praise it was the Swiss master Conrad Ferdinand

Meyer. On reading the first half, this connoisseur singled it out as "probably the most superb thing the *Rundschau* has *ever* brought out in the pure art form of the novel: finely wrought psychology, clear contours, extremely true-to-life characters and over everything nevertheless a certain poetic aura" (HF I/2, 985). Otto Brahm, a leader of the new generation, placed the seventy-two-year-old "youthful old-timer" ("der jugendliche Alte") in the company of the acknowledged masters of the age, asserting, "A romantic element still rings on in him, and the modern resounds forcefully along with it . . . just as in Ibsen and Zola the symbolic overshadows and deepens reality, so too in Fontane the old and the new come together, the balladesque and the impressionistic" (AA I/6, 486).

Yet negative tones have been heard as well. It has been argued that the punishment accorded Holk is scarcely in keeping with the magnitude of his crime, and that given her religious nature, Christine's suicide does not seem credible. Wandrey reckoned *Unwiederbringlich* the best of Fontane's secondary works, a position it seems to have maintained until the appearance of Demetz's *Formen des Realismus,* where it was singled out as "Fontane's most flawless artwork—devoid of slush or sentimentality, cool, composed, controlled, a book entirely of ivory, the only German novel of the epoch which need not fear competition even with Turgenev, or with Trollope and William Dean Howells" (Demetz, 166). With this accolade began a procession of studies of various aspects of the novel, by no means, however, without critical objectivity.

Why then has *Unwiederbringlich* remained in the shadow of *Irrungen, Wirrungen, Frau Jenny Treibel,* and *Effi Briest,* a work reserved for, as Demetz (Demetz, 165) puts it, the happy few? He provides one answer: German literary criticism, in its Hegelian origins, finds no real handle for coming to grips with a novel so devoid of political or historical ballast. Whether the book is truly without such elements is, as noted, by no means agreed upon. Certainly its locale places it outside the horizons of many German readers' interests, including those of not a few scholars and critics.

A far more obvious reason lies in the characters themselves. The old truism of plot and character as the determinants of a work's enduring success holds. The situation described by Fontane may indeed be archetypical: the middle-aged man, alienated from a no longer youthful wife, temporarily restored through infatuation with a younger woman, only to realize too late his mistake, cast furthermore in an adroitly fashioned psychological-symbolic matrix. Yet in all her rectitude, Christine alienates not only her husband. As for Holk, even if we sympathize with his irritation at the haughty religiosity of his spouse or with his playing into the arms of a bored coquette, he is scarcely an admirable figure; he is, rather, a hapless fool. Although Fontane strives to depict them as positively as possible, there is in the end little that is winning about Christine, Ebba, or Holk. The reader who might be eager for more of Botho and Lene, Frau Dörr and Käthe, Widow Pittelkow, Effi, or even Innstetten is, I believe, even if deeply moved by their tragedy, not a little glad to be done with the residents of the castle on the dunes.

Chapter Six
Romantic Regressions: Late Morality Tales

Fontane had written *Grete Minde* and *Ellernklipp* relatively early in his career as a fiction writer. As we have seen, financial factors were important in their production. As shorter works, they were more quickly placed in popular literary magazines and offered a speedier monetary return. Devoted to the psychological exploration of criminal events, they were also more in keeping with the demands of the conventional genre of the German novella, which from Kleist on had shown a predilection for the violent personality. In the latter half of the 1880s, he returned to the genre at the behest of the popular middle-class magazine *Die Gartenlaube* to write two more such works, *Unterm Birnbaum* and *Quitt*.

There can be no question that Fontane's crime stories taken as a whole are his weakest works. Essentially antiquarian in setting and romantic morality tales in conception, they obviously represent a throwback to conventional literary origins and, with the exception of *Quitt,* essentially lie outside the sociocritical area for which Fontane is esteemed. Yet as Hubert Ohl has pointed out, they are deserving of serious consideration, for in them, "in the thematic complexes of guilt and atonement, social morality and religiously grounded individual conscience, the free act of the individual and an enigmatically prevailing fate, an area of conflict becomes visible which Fontane perhaps more artfully submerged in his great social novels but which he by no means denied."[1]

Unterm Birnbaum

Despite its problematic ending, *Unterm Birnbaum* stands head and shoulders above the others in the group. In this highly moralistic tale, the lesson of which is the admittedly rather trivial idea that regardless of how fine a web of deceit we spin, "murder will out," Fontane also poured consummate skill into character presentation and the description of milieu and atmosphere. As a realistic presentation of the people and mores of the territory of the Oderbruch, the western side of the Oder River valley east of Berlin between Oderberg and Kustrin (Kostrzyn, now Poland), during the first third of the nineteenth century, the work is a minor masterpiece.

The region was familiar to the author. From 1838 to 1850 his father had owned an apothecary shop in the village of Letschin. Between 1843 and 1847 he vacationed there or worked on and off in his father's shop and in 1847 prepared for his final examination in pharmacy in Letschin. During these periods he had ample opportunity to study the locale and its inhabitants, some of whom appear with remarkable detail in the story written four decades later of an innkeeper and his wife who murder a traveling salesman for money and, despite elaborate efforts to prevent the truth from coming to light, are ultimately destroyed by the consequences of their crime.

Much of the story seems to have been written in the autumn of 1884. Corrections carried into the spring of the next year and the work appeared in *Die Gartenlaube* from August to September of 1885. A book edition followed in November 1885 as Volume 23 in a series devoted to contemporary authors offered by the Berlin publishing house of Müller-Grote.

Unterm Birnbaum is neither a detective story of the whodunit variety nor a crime story based on the psychological investigation of the motives behind a criminal act. Nor are many of the conventional attributes of mystery/crime tales to be found here. The motivation is transparent early in the story. Although the authorial viewpoint is manipulated to keep the reader more or less in the dark as to the actual events, it is not difficult to piece together the action. The reader's nerves are scarcely titillated, and little in the way of fear or excitement is generated. The murder itself is not even described secondhand; indeed, the reader does not even learn how the victim actually died. Planning and the murder itself are completed by the end of chapter 7 so that the remaining 20 chapters are given over to the efforts of the chief perpetrator to assist the bungling authorities to prevent the discovery of the crime. Thus it is not the murder itself and its solution that provide the main plot of the story, but again the psychological factor, the study of the desire to commit the perfect crime, and the final undoing of the criminal by forces unclear even at the end.

The story is based on an actual event that occurred in Letschin in 1842. During the construction of sidewalks for which sand was taken from the garden of a local hotel, a skeleton was discovered. Suspicion fell on the owner and his wife in connection with the disappearance of a grain salesman who had spent the night in their establishment and was never seen again, although his wagon was found in the Oder. Although no proof that a crime had been committed was forthcoming, the innkeeper fell into debt, sold the property, and came to a miserable end in a nearby town. His wife and children emigrated to America.

For color, Fontane set his tale in the early 1830s, incorporating aspects of the Polish uprising against Russia that had fascinated him since boyhood. Indeed, a host of youthful memories seem to have gone into the work, not only in the depiction of locale and secondary characters, but in the personages of the protagonist Hradscheck and his wife. In their differences early in the story they suggest the tensions between the author's own parents. At the same time their backgrounds reflect something of Fontane's Uncle August and Aunt Pinchen. Recalling the settlement of the Oderbruch in the 1740s by colonists from Bohemia under Frederick the Great, Letschin, in a variant of another village name of the region, appears as Tschechin.

Sociological, economic, and psychological factors leave no question that Hradscheck and his wife are in desperate straits. Countless touches reveal Fontane's skill at showing character. A slack administrator—his grain sacks are poorly tied, for instance—Hradscheck is also not given to emotionalizing death, even that of his children. Yet he is not unlikable. In fact, Fontane shows him to be a solicitous and loving husband who desperately wishes his wife better days. Both a hale fellow and boon companion, he is at the same time a canny judge of his neighbors' prejudices and gullibility.

Hradscheck's wife Ursel, on the other hand, far less clever and calculating than her husband and a typical Fontane outsider, is desperately afraid of poverty, and thus quickly won over to her husband's plan to murder a traveling salesman. Vain and pretentious, with a taste for material comforts, which are also in part responsible for their situation, she is the weakest link in his enterprise, for—like Franziska Franz and Cécile—she is an uneasy woman with a deep sense of religious yearning, which has led her to convert from Catholicism to Protestantism. Spiritual turmoil resulting from her part in the crime, ignored by the fatuous and undiscerning pastor Eccelius, another exemplar of an ineffectual clergyman, ultimately proves her undoing. Her inability to come to terms with her guilt undermines her health and soon leads to her death.

Hradscheck's primary antagonist is Mutter Jeschke, a witch-like old crone reminiscent of Hoppchen Marie in *Vor dem Sturm*. With her probing and equivocal allusions to mysterious forces and the happenings in his house, it is she who in the end drives Hradscheck to give in to superstitious fears, despite his better judgment. But she is only one aspect of the setting. To no less an extent than in his best novels of Berlin high society, Fontane succeeds in *Unterm Birnbaum* in depicting the texture of the society of a remote Prussian village in the days of Friederich Wilhelm III. The fickleness of public opinion, backbiting, gossip, jealousy, avarice, and slander go hand in hand with the callousness, carelessness, and stupidity of local authorities in assuring the success of Hradscheck's scheme.

To those for whom Fontane represents a consummate realist, the conclusion of *Unterm Birnbaum* presents a problem. An intricate case history is presented in which social and psychological factors dominate. Superstition and fear of discovery are functioning elements in the overall portrait of characters and locale as part of the work's psychological verisimilitude. Nevertheless, Hradscheck's death at the spot where he has buried his victim, interpreted for the reader by Pastor Eccelius in the sententious statement "No web's so finely spun, everything comes to the light of the sun" (HF I/1, 554), seems to be nothing but romantic fatalism, positing an order of retribution inconsistent with the social criticism on which the story is otherwise founded.

"Practically any other conclusion might have offered itself, but not this one," writes Müller-Seidel, who argues that Hradscheck's survival as a wealthy man, well-regarded by the community, would have been far more in keeping with the tone of the story (Müller-Seidel, 227). Yet it is evident that Fontane viewed his story in precisely opposite terms; a letter to Georg Friedlaender attests to his conviction that elements of beauty, consolation, and ennoblement tread invisibly through the story, representing "the proclaimed gospel of the justice of God, of the order in His world."[2] Like all Fontane's crime tales, *Unterm Birnbaum* represents an aspect of the author's worldview difficult to reconcile with the skeptic of Potsdamer Straße 134c, especially for those who would prefer to see a unified picture of evolution from romantic categories of crime and punishment to the empirical objectivity of the revered social critic. Yet fatalism and predestination remained inherent categories of Fontane's entire oeuvre and he never became the complete objectivist some would make of him. Thus for all its finely crafted verisimilitude, *Unterm Birnbaum* remains firmly enmeshed in the Weltanschauung of Fontane the ballad writer, a stage that paradoxically the social critic and contemporary observer only seemingly outgrew.

Quitt

Quitt was written at the request of *Die Gartenlaube* following the success of *Unterm Birnbaum*. A topic was at hand. During his summer 1884 stay at Krummhübel in the Silesian Riesengebirge, Fontane had learned of the murder of the forester Wilhelm Frey by a poacher named Knobloch, who had then fled to America. Returning to Krummhübel in June 1885, the writer set to work almost immediately. Correspondence makes it clear that from the outset he envisioned a novel of crime and atonement that would conclude in a Mennonite colony in the United States. Work on the story, which soon stretched to novel length, extended for several years until April 1889. Abridged with Fontane's approval, *Quitt* appeared in *Die Gartenlaube* early in 1890, and, dated 1891, was published in the autumn in its complete form by Wilhelm Hertz.

From its first appearance, *Quitt* has been considered an inferior work. "Whoever has not already done so should calmly let *Quitt* remain unread and in its place open *Irrungen, Wirrungen* for a second or third time," maintained Karl Emil Franzos (AA I/V, 628), who complained about its weakness of characterization and the deficit of local color throughout. Although some modern critics, including Demetz, have been more positively disposed, Helmut Nürnberger (*TF in Selbstzeugnissen*, 133ff.) speaks for the majority in maintaining that *Quitt*, along with all Fontane's crime stories, is artistically a second class product, tailored to the expectations of readers of the *Gartenlaube*, and written "counter to his talent, as well as counter to his understanding of his talent."

Yet it will not do to dismiss the novel out of hand. Although obviously flawed, both psychologically and as a document of social criticism, its first half richly deserves Müller-Seidel's accolade as "ein kleines Meisterwerk" (Müller-Seidel 299). Indeed, *Quitt* is unique among Fontane's crime stories for its political ramifications; it contains the sharpest judgments against the German Empire to be found in Fontane's fiction, in part justifying its mention among the works covered in chapter 4.

The first part of *Quitt* takes place in the Krummhübel region of Silesia (now in Poland). The hotheaded 27-year-old cartwright Lehnert Menz has for several years feuded with the local forester, Opitz, who regards Menz's independent and haughty ways as insolent disrespect for his authority and has already seen to it that Lehnert has spent two months in jail. Despite the efforts of various secondary characters to prevent it, a final clash is inevitable as the symbolic juxtaposition of their houses, facing each other across a narrow river, suggests. A trivial episode precipitates the catastrophe. When Lehnert denies shooting a rabbit from the game preserve on his land, Opitz in a show of lenience offers to overlook the act provided Lehnert apologizes for his lie. Lehnert naturally refuses and, knowing that he will be jailed for a second time, decides to deal with his antagonist once and for all. Disguised and with loaded shotgun, he seeks a confrontation in the mountains.

Lehnert is not a cold-blooded killer, however. He seeks to avoid ultimate responsibility and to ameliorate his guilt by leaving it to God's judgment whether he will encounter his antagonist. But rejecting such rationalization as inherently cowardly, he instead decides to tempt fate by choosing the path he expects Opitz will take. At the crucial instant, however, the forester attempts to fire first, bringing in the question of self-defense. Opitz's gun misfires and Lehnert brings him down. Moreover, Lehnert ratifies his act the next day by not responding to a cry he knows comes from the wounded man. When, after the body is discovered, suspicion turns on him, he flees.

After an interpolated six-year interval during which we are informed that Lehnert has made and lost a fortune in California, the action turns to the Indian Territory south of Kansas. There a matured and wiser Menz encounters a colony of Mennonites he had run across earlier. He works for a time on their farm, and finally joins the group. Proving himself, he asks to marry the leader's daughter, Ruth. On an excursion to the nearby hills he saves Ruth's life and his request is granted. Fate intervenes. On a solitary mission to rescue her brother in the nearby mountains he is seriously injured and, like Optiz, dies alone. In his own blood he leaves a last message, asking forgiveness and hoping that his debt has been made *quitt,* paid in full.

Although striking the modern reader as a highly contrived work, the initial half of *Quitt* provides a convincing portrait of the inexorable conflict between two men who in stubbornness and inflexibility are, as one of the chorus of onlookers notes, essentially similar (HF I/1, 229). Destiny has put them in different positions within the hierarchy of this provincial corner of Bismarck's Reich. As the representative of civic order, the Prussian *Obrigkeit,* Opitz will tolerate no violation of his authority or position as a *Respektsperson.* A classic example of the petty tyrant such a system inevitably fosters, when it comes to himself

Opitz is self-indulgent. With others, however, he is exacting and arbitrary in the exercise of his authority, holding unyieldingly to the traditional Prussian military values of order, duty, and obedience. Thus he regards the individualistic Menz as an arrogant inferior and a representative of forces hostile to the Reich.

Lehnert Menz, on the other hand, is equally touchy and deeply embittered. He has not forgotten that it was Opitz who prevented his receiving the Iron Cross for gallantry during the war and who has already had him imprisoned. At the same time, it is not merely a personal conflict. The forester has become for Lehnert the personification of an insufferable system, the Prussianized authoritarian *Obrigkeitsstaat* from which he yearns to liberate himself. "It's so small and narrow for me here," he tells his mother. "A police state, a land with a few masters and counts like ours here, but otherwise with nothing but flunkies and servants" (HF I/1, 261).

It is not only in Lehnert's embittered remarks that Fontane's critique of the Reich may be found. In a variety of ways the book deals with the deficiencies of Bismarck's state, exposing its inherent militarism and authoritarianism, and its creation of a society of narrow-minded provincials, petty tyrants, hypocrites, and bootlickers. Siebenhaar, the village pastor, for instance, who has a soft spot in his heart for Lehnert, nevertheless stays safely on the side of state authority, law and order. Without naming him, he unmistakably denounces Lehnert's behavior from the pulpit while talking to the equally culpable Opitz in private. An old nationalist from his student days, he lectures Lehnert on his democratic inclinations, telling him, "And now you're even reading all sorts of stupid papers in which arrogant schoolmasters and lying pettifoggers show off their wares, and are going around in all the inns talking about freedom and the republic and America, the happy land. Lehnert, Lehnert, I've always thought you were too good for that sort of thing!" (HF I/1, 218).

In a scene both comic and bitterly satirical of the Prussian militaristic tone that infects even the most provincial corners of the Reich, the man of God tearfully thanks Heaven for having lived to see the day when he encounters the uniformed village fire department saluting him as they march by with military pomp. Similarly, another response to the authoritarianism characteristic of the German state is the groveling servility combined with cunning opportunism exhibited by Lehnert's mother, which her son for obvious reasons finds so repulsive.

Especially revealing are the interspersed episodes dealing with *Rechnungsrat* (Auditor), later *Geheimrat* (Privy Councilor), Espe, who with his family appears at crucial junctures to interject self-satisfied bourgeois moral comments. As the reader soon learns, Espe and his family are by no means all that they appear, and although ostentatiously retaining the mantle of respectability, it is obvious that Espe's success has been based on the principle of getting along by going along.

It is worth noting, too, that in his desire to turn his back on Bismarck's Germany and seek his fortune in America, Lehnert Menz is the only Fontane character to criticize the Reich in uncompromising political terms. Others complain about the narrowness of their personal lives under Wilhelmine social and moral strictures, but only Lehnert rails against the prevailing atmosphere of subservience and servility demanded of those whose place is on the lower rungs of the social ladder. "You've always got to dance attendance on somebody," he argues, "and when you bow down frontwards, you knock over somebody in the rear" (HF I/1, 261).

That Fontane has Menz do what many of his other figures only talk of doing—leave the Reich for America—proved for the author a serious miscalculation. What was said of *Graf Petöfy,* that despite his research Fontane knew too little about the country and its people, is doubly valid for *Quitt*. The problem is all the more acute in that the milieu of the first part is so rich in convincing detail. By comparison, the latter half, based on foreign sources—Fontane drew on the reminiscences of the critic Paul Lindau, who had crossed the United States by rail, and on various Mennonite periodicals available to him in Germany—is unconvincing and pale. This section, in which the hero leaves his Silesian homeland to find refuge in an American Mennonite settlement in the Indian Territory of what later became Arkansas, makes hard demands on the credulity of even the most sympathetic modern reader. In the colony, which is named after a tributary of the Vistula and bears the improbable name of Nogat-Ehre (Nogat-Honor), Mentz is surrounded by figures with even more unlikely names, ranging from the group leader, Obadja Hornbostel, to an Indian Chief called Gunpowder Face and a dog named Uncas. Distances too are unrealistic and the Ozark mountain landscape, a few American names notwithstanding, remains resolutely German. Apart from Indians, who are depicted almost as children in their eagerness to acquire European ways, the atmosphere of the settlement is heavily Teutonic, even to the stag's antler chandelier decorating the main hall. German customs and culture dominate the conversation, while the American scene, in which, after all, Lehnert has been involved for more than six years, despite pictures of George Washington and Ulysses S. Grant, is hardly convincingly portrayed. It has been shown that most of the names and places used by Fontane, including some of the more outlandish ones, were in fact associated with the Mennonite colony at Darlington in the Arkansas Indian Territory.[3] Nevertheless, their garishly exotic extravagance along with the wan utopianism of the Mennonite group, as Fontane presents it, seem hardly believable.

Every bit as debilitating, however, is the heavy-handed fatalism injected into the conclusion. In the first half of the novel, psychological verisimilitude and inevitability are convincingly interwoven. The conflict beween the self-righteous and rebellious individualist Menz and the self-important petty official Opitz is presented as an inexorably predestined chain of events. Not so the outcome. It is true that the view that a certain law determines human existence is an inherent trait of Fontane's ouevre. As we have seen, fatalism can be traced from *Vor dem Sturm* to *Effi Briest*. Despite the skeptical leanings that led him to a more materialistically oriented realism in his later years, it is a legacy of Fontane's Calvinist background and of the balladesque romanticism of his formative years that he never fully eschewed. In his best works, its workings are suggested rather than sententiously depicted. Yet Lehnert's death comes, as it were, out of the blue. Menz's friend, L'Hermite, a fugitive from the Paris Commune, offers comments which are obviously intended to prepare the reader for the outcome. "There is such a thing as fate," he tells Lehnert. "And because there is such a thing as fate, everything follows its path, darkly and enigmatically, and it's only now and then that a ray of light flashes and lets us see just enough to get an idea of the moods and the laws of the powers that are eternal and enigmatic, or whatever else you want to call them" (HF I/1, 429). Yet even after such obvious groundwork, the parallel between Lehnert's end and Opitz's death is unconvincing. Although in the final analysis it is Lehnert himself and no one else who endows his end with exculpatory significance, not unlike the outcome of Schiller's *Maria Stuart*, there is also at work in *Quitt* a sententious and creaking eye-for-an-eye justice. It is a force left over from the romantic fate tragedies *Ellernklipp* and *Unterm Birnbaum*, implying that no crime will go unpunished, and that retribution will be had, be it by human or unknown hand. Such moralizing may have been suited to the comfortable middle-class readers of the *Gartenlaube,* but in a work in which psychology has played such a determining role, its presence can only leave the reader astonished.

Chapter Seven
Adeldämmerung: Dilemmas of a Dying Class

Fontane's last two novels could easily be classified among the Berlin novels. Yet certain aspects of theme and structure set *Die Poggenpuhls* (1896) and *Der Stechlin* (1898) somewhat apart. Continuing a tendency begun in *Frau Jenny Treibel,* they are no longer works in which the psychological exploration of a violation of the social or moral code is the principal tectonic element. Instead, they offer static presentations of a dilemma close to the author's heart—the plight of the Prussian aristocracy in the German Reich as the century drew to its close. They also exhibit unconventionalities that have led some to dismiss them as manifestations of the declining powers of their aged author.

Fontane always had a warm regard for the Prussian nobility, especially its older generations. In the best of the old families of the Mark Brandenburg he perceived the virtues that had created and sustained Prussia's greatness. Above all, the Junkers on their provincial estates embodied for him a unique mixture of consciousness of duty and the easygoing sophistication and blithe gentility utterly lacking in the ostentatious and avaricious bourgeoisie then taking over the rapidly expanding capital and, by virtue of patents of nobility acquired through wealth, even displacing the manor-born as the cultural foundation of the Reich.

With time, however, he had come to recognize that his predilection for the titled had outlived itself. Especially in private letters to Georg Friedlaender he expressed himself uncompromisingly concerning the aristocracy. Their relentless hold on privilege, their selfishness and lack of political vision led him to the realization that the nobility could not and did not deserve to survive without substantive change. In his fiction, however, he was more circumspect. The sense of the poetic that Fontane found inherent in the way of life of the titled still guided his pen in his last two works. Now, however, a new aspect made itself felt, and the life of the Prussian nobility is presented in an autumnal poetry of decline and demise.

Die Poggenpuhls

Fontane's penultimate story chronicles a historical inevitability of the Second Reich, the extinction of the lowest ranks of the nobility. Anachronistically continuing to dominate in military and diplomatic spheres, the Prussian aristocracy, which represented only one percent of the population, was nevertheless rapidly rendered economically irrelevant by industrialization and capitalism. As an ethic of work and wealth supplanted birth and privilege as the standard of social and cultural status, more and more blue-blooded families found themselves forced to the margins of society. The lower ranks of the so-called *Schwertadel* (military aristocracy), which had led the Prussian army since the days of the Soldier King, apart from their tattered decorations and small, inefficient estates, possessed little in the way of wealth. Their position, based on military service to the Hohenzollern crown, rapidly dissipated. The blood of massed infantry battalions supplanted individual gallantry. Similarly, the iron forged by a sweating proletariat in foundries where birth gave way to brute strength now provided the weapons that had become the new pillars of Prussia's military success. Family honor and the consciousness of having served king and country proved scarcely adequate lines of defense in the new social struggle in which money had become the primary means of staying on top.

Die Poggenpuhls alternated with *Mathilde Möhring, Meine Kinderjahre,* and *Effi Briest* on Fontane's desk from 1891 until the summer of 1894. Offered to the weekly *Daheim,* in which *Vor dem Sturm* had appeared 16 years earlier, it was rejected for fear that the author's portrayal of the nobility might offend. Fontane angrily dismissed such an attitude in his journal, arguing somewhat speciously that *Die Poggenpuhls* represented "a glorification of the nobility," which, he felt compelled to add, "feels things in a stupid and petty enough way that it won't perceive the flattering things in it" (HF I/4, 819). It was first published in *Vom Fels zum Meer* (From the cliffs to the sea) in the autumn and spring of 1895–96. The book appeared under the imprint of Friedrich Fontane in November 1896.

The plot is thin. A down-at-the-heels aristocratic family in a shabby apartment in Berlin celebrates their widowed mother's birthday. A visit to the theater with a presumably rich uncle provides an interesting digression in the company of a nobleman-turned-actor. At the uncle's request, the middle daughter accompanies him to his estate, where she employs her artistic skills in decorating the local church and acts as companion to him and his wife. Unexpectedly, the uncle dies. His widow provides the family with a modest allowance, and the wolf is kept from the family door for another day.

The initial chapters, describing the family's circumstances and providing introductory characterizations, deserve to be reckoned among Fontane's finest. Even their living quarters on Großgorschenstraße are symbolic. Tombstones and hereditary vaults in a cemetery outside their front windows point both to their future and to the moribund heroic tradition associated with the family's past, while, visible from the rear of their apartment, the garish sign of a candy factory proclaims the tastelessness of the new era that is about to overtake them. In another symbolic touch, they survive by virtue of the charitable indulgence of a former foot soldier in the major's old battalion in one of the dwellings thrown up in Berlin during the boom of the early 1880s, as *Trockenwohner,* occupants paying reduced rates because wet plaster was considered unhealthy. Their family name, Poggenpuhl, essentially a dialect word meaning frog-puddle, comically suggests their true significance in Prussian affairs. So do the few things they have salvaged from better times, especially the paintings depicting moments of family glory. Whatever heroism may reside in the canvas of a last-ditch stand by a Poggenpuhl ancestor, obscured by gunsmoke, incongruously bootless and clad only in his underwear and waistcoat, who attempts to hold off an overwhelming enemy during one of Frederick the Great's defeats, is reduced to comedy when the picture falls from the crumbling wall at nearly every attempt to dust it. In fact, the picture is doubly symbolic; it also suggests the vain rearguard defense of the present ill-prepared generation, engaged in a holding action they cannot win, as they are about to fall from their place in German society. Threadbare curtains, barren rooms, bare floors, and make-do sleeping arrangements all attest to the desperate straits into which the von Poggenpuhls have fallen, eking out an existence, as Leo, the youngest Poggenpuhl son, describes them, "in a kind of perfection," the "pure species" of impoverished aristocracy (HF I/4, 490).

Affection touched with irony and even a bit of malice, along with a wit foreshadowing Thomas Mann's, come to the fore as Fontane delineates the family's inner circle. Suggestively enthroned in a rocking chair, Therese, the snobbish eldest sister, a caricature on a par with Jenny Treibel, staunchly maintains their shredded dignity with unquenchable hauteur. Sophie, the appropriately named middle daughter, is characterized as a new breed of noblewoman in the Darwinian struggle for social existence, one who displays something hitherto disdained by most aristocratic families—practical talents. The youngest Poggenpuhl, Manon, lacking any utilitarian skills, has nevertheless found the most useful role of all, as a titled doll who brightens the drawing rooms of the ascendant bourgeoisie and at the same time assures her more gifted sister of an outlet for her abilities. In his trio of Poggenpuhl graces, Fontane lightly caricatures several modes of the threadbare lower nobility's acclimation to Bismarck's new Germany: the unrealistic unwillingness of some to accept marginalization on the one hand, the readiness of others to compromise with bourgeois standards if need be, or to parasitically lend legitimacy to the pretentions of the nouveau riche through the prestige, grace, and aura of good taste associated with their old family names.

In keeping with family tradition, both of the von Poggenpuhl sons, Leo and Wendelin, are officers. One of the nuances of the work is the absence of the eldest, Wendelin. From what we learn of him, he seems to be the most uncharacteristic Poggenpuhl, one who blends the family's military heritage with his mother's bourgeois background. The outcome seems to be the typically Prussian *Streber,* a relentless striver, single-mindedly devoted to duty and goals. By birth and tradition an officer, Wendelin von Poggenpuhl is nevertheless a careerist, intent on advancement, a participant in the unremitting militarism permeating the new Reich in which the application of German industriousness and thoroughness creates a new mode of faceless total war utterly at odds with the ethos of gallantry associated with past generations. In its place, an impersonal force of massed transport, Krupp artillery barrages, Mauser rifles, and Schlieffen plans rises, an example of what the writer criticized in the military as a sign of inner decay, "selfishness and the most ruthless striving," qualities that had taken the place of "a fine sense of honor and aristocratic gentility."[1] It is a keen irony that the professional military scholar Wendelin is precisely the type of modern strategist who renders the single-handed heroics of the past, by which the Poggenpuhl women hope Leo will rejuvenate the family's prestige, utterly impossible. "Standing in front and shouting hurrah don't mean much to him," Leo writes his sister, "he is for strategic ideas" (HF I/4, 549).

In contrast, through Leo and General Eberhard von Poggenpuhl, the author pays compliment to two types he traditionally associated with the nobility: the dashingly irresponsible young officer—his own son

Georg is considered to have been the model—and in the general, the affable aristocrat of the old school, cordial, unpretentious and, with the wisdom of years, aware of the inevitability of change. Leo, for all his superficial frivolity, is not without substance. A good deal of despair lies at the bottom of his easy ways, for it is he who recognizes most clearly the family's plight. His noncommittal response to Therese's assertion regarding the emperor's recognition of the value of the Poggenpuhls speaks volumes. Similarly, in a discussion with Manon he points out to her without illusion that the Poggenpuhls' claim to fame is based on values no longer current: It is not the old names rich with associations in Prussian history that count in the modern world but instead the utterly prosaic ones of commerce and material comfort; the *Litfassäule,* advertising pillars present on every Berlin street and aimed at the lowest common cultural denominator, have replaced the heroic equestrian monument as the symbol of the new German Empire.

Another indication of the new era's break with the past, however, is seen in the evening spent with Herr von Klessentin, following a visit to the theater to watch von Wildenbruch's *Die Quitzows.* In that immensely popular work of the 1880s, the pre-Hohenzollern Prussian aristocracy and its role in the creation of the Prussian state were turned into theatrical pageantry. Yet reverence for the heroic was already a casualty in the mass culture of the Reich. The theatergoers must choose between the actual drama or a popular parody of it. Recognizing only too well the implications of each for family and caste, General von Poggenpuhl chooses the serious version as the less offensive alternative.

Even at the theater there is little room for illusion. In Leo's friend von Klessentin, an irony that does not escape the general, a nobleman is reduced to being a bit player in the historical pageant of his titled forebears. On the threshold of becoming déclassé, Herr von Klessentin has become Herr Manfred. One cannot in the long run hope for much better for the Poggenpuhl women either. Their future lies not on the stage but in the drawing rooms of the well-to-do as ladies' companions and governesses. The likelihood that they or their brothers will find suitable matches to ensure the family's future is small. With the sudden death of the general passes an age and implicitly a class.

Compositionally, *Die Poggenpuhls* seems to be one of Fontane's more impoverished efforts. The delightful beginning, with its conversational exchanges and appealing and imaginative characters, is abandoned half way through in favor of an epistolary segment that takes the book in a direction scarcely foreseeable at the outset, and is inappropriately matched with the whimsical tone of the beginning. Wandrey (Wandrey, 298) notes the disappointment of readers' expectations regarding Leo's future. Moreover, the outcome of the novel, scarcely a miracle of the sort Leo has facetiously hoped for, is unconvincingly left to a kind of seminoble deus ex machina in the personage of an aunt who is introduced only toward the end. True, the ending generally brings the novel more or less back on track. The passing of the elder Poggenpuhl, however, despite its symbolic connotations, strikes the reader as strangely sudden—especially for a writer so skilled in formal anticipation as was Fontane. At moments, although his sketches make evident that this was not the case, it is as if the author had begun one book and ended with another.

What is missed in such comments is the work's ultimate meaning. In the apparent inertia of both form and content lies its primary message: The story of the marginalized nobility is no story; it exhausts itself in characterization. Attractive though they may be as individuals, the Poggenpuhls as a family and as a historical force have become passé. Nothing has prepared them for the world in which they now find themselves, and the world does not care. Even their familial estates, once the basis of their continued existence, are now only memories experienced indirectly through the medium of letters. Their survival, once guaranteed by their title, has indeed become a matter of signs and wonders.

At the same time, in the figures of both the Frau Generalin and the Frau Majorin, neither of whom is a born aristocrat, Fontane suggests anew a belief, expressed earlier in the character of Marie in *Vor dem Sturm,* that true nobility is a matter of character rather than of birth. Through them, as Therese gradually recognizes, the best qualities of the Prussian nobility—generosity, loyalty, and humanitarianism—have by no means died out but may continue to survive in an aristocracy of heart rather than of birth.

There is a negative side to *Die Poggenpuhls* that we can scarcely ignore. Diametrically opposed to the gallant but historically irrelevant Poggenpuhls are the Bartensteins, an up-and-coming Jewish family, obviously ascending the social ladder as the former slip ever lower. For Fontane, of course, scorn for the bourgeois and anti-Semitism were but two sides of the same skeptical attitude towards what he saw as the coarseness and materialism that had established themselves in the new Reich. Yet modern readers cannot help but be troubled by the inferences in the novel which make clear that the horrors of the twentieth century did not come out of thin air.[2]

Fontane was aware of the book's structural problems. To Freidrich Spielhagen, the contemporary authority on novel structure, he lamely sought to excuse them, arguing that the novel's "programmatic aspect, the setting up of schematic outlines for the characters, who then later appear, and, to top it off, breaking off the narrative to continue at a later point with letters, is admittedly a flaw, but I should like to be permitted to say that (if the whole thing was to remain brief) in this way I have avoided even larger flaws."[3] Perhaps. But as we have seen, the intervening segments dealing with Sophie's exploits in Silesia, although not unrelated to the primary theme, contribute little to brevity and leave too much of what was promisingly begun frustratingly unresolved.

And yet, if from a formal standpoint *Die Poggenpuhls* is one of Fontane's most unsatisfying works, as people the Poggenpuhls are among his most winning creations. "The individual above all!" he wrote a critic. "The book is not a novel and has no content, its 'how' has to take the place of its 'what.'"[4] Thus the chief charm of this little book lies in its characters. It is a tale in which extinction is bathed in a slightly nostalgic poetic aura. If not the glorification he termed it, nevertheless in the entire Poggenpuhl clan as he depicted it in the novel, Fontane creates a memorial to the gentility and grace of the best of the Prussian nobility, who even in the face of ruin maintained an air of self-esteem and refinement, "proof to the world that, even in the most modest circumstances, as long as the right attitude, and of course, the necessary skillfulness as well were supplied, that one could live contentedly and almost as befits one's station" (HF I/4, 482). Moreover, through its continuing popularity, Fontane's penultimate novel is proof that it is not always aesthetic perfection which assures a work its place in the literary canon so much as it is its richness of characterization.

Der Stechlin

In the autumn of 1895 Fontane shelved a long-planned historical-political novel, *Die Likedeeler* (The equal sharers), about the fifteenth-century pirate Stortebecker, whose band he envisioned as a revolutionary protocommunistic society, in favor of "a small political novel" (HF I/5, 417) of contemporary life that urged itself on him. Working intensely, the 76-year-old had the first draft of *Der Stechlin* on paper by year's end. Aware, as he expressed it, that he was looking towards sunset, Fontane immediately set to rewriting. Despite the author's increasing infirmities, the "small political novel" burgeoned into a large one and was completed by summer of 1897. The esteem he now enjoyed as the grand old man of German letters enabled Fontane to pass over the parsimonious *Deutsche Rundschau,* in which *Unwiederbringlich, Frau Jenny Treibel,* and *Effi Briest* had initially appeared, and to place the novel under more favorable conditions. A special announcement and photo of the "aged but youthfully fresh author"[5] previewed *Der Stechlin*'s appearance between October and December 1897 in the illustrated journal *Über Land und Meer* (O'er land and sea). A second volume of memoirs, *Zwischen Zwanzig und Dreißig* (Between twenty and thirty), along with revisions for the book edition of *Der Stechlin* occupied him throughout the spring and summer of 1898. At his death a list of those who were to receive review copies of the yet unreleased edition of *Der Stechlin* lay on his desk. Dated 1899, the work was brought out in October 1898, some four weeks after Fontane's death, by his son's publishing house. Reviews, by and large cast as eulogies of the writer, were generally favorable.

The novel's architecture is unusual. "Not a trace is to be found of tension or surprises, complications or the resolution of love conflicts or conflicts of any sort" (HF I/5, 420), admitted the author. At the same time he expressed his conviction that *Der Stechlin,* in which "various persons meet on the one hand on an old-fashioned estate in the Mark and on the other in the modern house of a count (Berlin) and talk over God and the world," and in which everything was "dialogue and chit-chat . . . through which the characters reveal themselves," represented "not just the right way, but even the obligatory way to write a novel of the age."[6] Once more, stylistic traits employed in *Die Poggenpuhls,* in which the *how* of the work substitutes for its *what,* clearly represented to Fontane's way of thinking a conscious formal development.

The plot is characterized by the author as "simply an idea in disguise. . . . at the end an old timer dies and two youngsters get married."[7] Implicit in its simple scheme, of course, is the eternal cycle of death and renewal, an end but also a beginning. Yet it must be conceded that *Der Stechlin* exhibits a certain slackening of structural control. Like *Die Poggenpuhls,* it has been viewed as the work of a comfortably self-indulgent old gentleman who was no longer able to rein in a proclivity to ramble. Yet it is difficult to agree with those who dismiss the work as the product of declining powers. A continued mastery of conversational style as well as an adroit use of symbolism and structural nuance still reveal the hand of the master. Present in larger measure than in any other work is a sense of Fontanean whimsy. Demetz's characterization of its essential structure as "additive" (Demetz, 179) is on the mark. Also correct, it must be admitted, is his assertion that the septuagenarian at times pushed his narrator out of the way to interpolate extended vignettes such as the story of the widow Schickedanz, or of Dr. Pusch, neither of which materially advance the story.

But these are disputable blemishes. From another point of view, they can be regarded not as flaws but as parts of the social pageant in which, as Eda Sagarra (Sagarra, 9) has pointed out, Fontane provides a subtly drawn portrait of the entire German Reich under the young Wilhelm II. It is a picture encompassing almost all classes, from serving girls to minor officials, from artists to aristocrats. As may be expected, however, the center of focus is again the nobility and the crisis it faced as the Reich shifted from an outmoded neofeudalism to an urban industrial society.

As Fontane himself made clear, the plot of *Der Stechlin* is slight. Retired Major Dubslav von Stechlin's estate is situated in a quiet rural area on Lake Stechlin, part of a chain of lakes in northwestern Brandenburg. According to tradition, despite its remote location, whenever significant geological events occur in the outside world, geysers appear on the lake. On particularly earthshaking happenings, a red cockerel is even supposed to emerge from the depths and its crowing heard over the countryside. The visit of the old Junker's son, Woldemar, an officer in the Dragoon Guards in Berlin, with his comrades Czako and Rex, elicits Dubslav's inquiries regarding whom the younger Stechlin will choose to marry. Woldemar assures his father a decision is near. Woldemar's aunt, whom he visits on the way back to Berlin, the narrow-minded and prejudiced prioress of a half-abandoned Lutheran convent, also presses her nephew for a guarantee that the house of Stechlin will survive.

In Berlin Woldemar has become a regular visitor at the home of Count Barby, a retired diplomat who spent many years serving in England. His choice for a bride seems to be between the count's daughters, the charming and witty divorcée Melusine, and her younger sister, the more taciturn Armgard. Questions of social justice and the obligations of the nobility for the future come to the fore. Woldemar's tutor, the local parson Lorenzen, has attempted to inculcate liberal values in his pupil and after a diplomatic mission to London, Woldemar's choice falls on Armgard. The Barbys visit Castle Stechlin and cement the relationship between the two families. Melusine further discusses the cultural and social values of the Reich with Lorenzen and stresses the necessity of the acceptance of change. After Armgard and Woldemar leave on their honeymoon, Dubslav's health fails. Calmly he awaits death as he is visited daily by Agnes, the illegitimate grandchild of one of his villagers. On his passing Lorenzen eulogizes him: "He was the best we can be, a man and a child" (HF I/5, 378). Woldemar and Armgard return to initiate the future.

His lifelong regard for Prussian landed aristocrats radiantly infuses Fontane's portrayal of his chief figure, Dubslav von Stechlin. He is an amalgamation of the best attributes of the titled class encountered by the Brandenburg wanderer in decades spent as an observer of the Prussian scene. As a representative of an autocratic but more genteel social order, Dubslav is whimsically skeptical of the new age. "Everything's gone down hill," he ruefully complains, "and it keeps on going further down hill. That's what they call new times, just keep on going down hill" (HF I/5, 53). Industrialization and its consequences are anathema to him. With patriarchal assurance, he views the inhabitants of the nearby villages as his own, and ruminates with dismay on the glass retorts they produce for Germany's flourishing chemical industry and the latter's caustic effects on the environment. "That's the sign of our times nowadays, 'scorched or corroded.' And then when I consider that my Globsowers are joining right in and as cheerfully as can be, providing the tools for the great general world scorching, let me tell you, gentlemen, that gives me a twinge" (HF I/5, 69). Similarly the old autocrat's participation in what he regards as a "newfangled" process of democratization—through running for the Reichstag—is aristocratically minimal, and the failure of his candidacy comes as more of a relief than a defeat.

Yet Fontane endows the old nobleman with warmly humane and skeptical traits reminiscent of his own personality as well as of the charm and grace he cherished in his father. Beneath Stechlin's reactionary exterior lie an individualistic skepticism towards traditional sacred cows and an irony and amused mistrust of absolutes, such as the old Junker's propensity for paradox and his conviction that "there are no unassailable truths and if there are any, they are boring" (HF I/5, 10). Dubslav's death and obsequies, written when the author recognized that his own time was running out, can be counted as one of the most luminous extended passages in Fontane's oeuvre.

The counterfoil to Dubslav von Stechlin is Count von Barby, the father of the two young women, Melusine and Armgard, who figure as a possible bride for Dubslav's son, Woldemar. That both Count Barby and Dubslav should bear a resemblance to Bismarck, the greatest German of the age, underscores their substance as representatives of the Reich. Apart from his similarity to the Iron Chancellor, however, Count Barby is "like a twin brother" to Dubslav, sharing, as Woldemar assures us, "the same humane nature, the same affability, the same good humor" (HF I/5, 116), and especially an utter lack of selfishness. Separating the two aristocrats are differences in background and range of thought. Diplomatic service has provided the count with a sophistication and objectivity the provincial Junker can scarcely comprehend. England, with all its associations in Fontane's thinking, is the decisive factor differentiating the two, for it has endowed Barby with a critical eye for Prussian provincialism and inbred arrogance, expressed in a pet phrase of Fontane's, "that beyond the mountains there really are people too. And sometimes very different ones" (HF I/5, 117). Thus in Fontane's final portrait of the Prussian aristocracy as it ought to be, to the upright Brandenburg honesty and common-sense integrity of Dubslav is added the urbanity, sophistication, and cosmopolitanism of Barby.

As the best of their kind, Major von Stechlin and Count Barby stand in marked contrast to the other aristocratic figures in the novel. Through his caricatures of more typical aristocrats of the Reich under Wilhelm II, Fontane satirizes the decadence, stupidity, and selfishness that vitiated his hopes for them in the Germany to come. Thus in the newly ennobled businessman Gundermann, ostentatiously fearful of the rise of social democracy, and his hopelessly gauche spouse, we are given a comic portrayal of the worst of the new *Briefadel,* the patent nobility for whom commercial success had become a stepping-stone to titled superiority. At the same time, the fossilization of the oldest families of rank is mocked in the senile Lord of Alten-Friesack, who idiotically presides over the table at the banquet celebrating Dubslav's election defeat. Not content with that, however, in the figure of Ermyntrud, Princess of Ippe-Büchsenstein, who has renounced rank and privilege to enter into a mésalliance with the local chief forester, and with earnest Prussian devotion to duty remains almost continually pregnant, Fontane parodies both the sentimental silliness latent in an age given to such pseudoheroic posturing and the egalitarian fanaticism of some members of the first estate.

Most grotesque of all is Dubslav's "petrified" sister, Adelheid. Through her self-satisfied class-consciousness she is a realistic portrayal of the arrogance and provincialism characteristic of many reactionary Prussian blue bloods. In the barrenness of her existence, suggested by her name (Adel = noble, Heide = heath), her way of life, and the surroundings in which she lives, Fontane implies the future that such ossification must inevitably bring. For the modern reader, her hidebound xenophobic tirades, bigoted Lutheranism, and anti-intellectualism would more than once cross the line into the hilarious were it not for their sinister associations with twentieth century Germany. Representatives of the younger generation, such as Rex and Czako, reveal themselves as only marginally better. Frivolous and cynical, or rigorously conservative, both are profoundly caste-conscious blue bloods, scarcely men of substance to offer confidence in the German future.

That future is, however, promised in the union of the houses of Stechlin and Barby. Significantly, eros plays no role; Woldemar's search for a suitable bride has been essentially concluded before the book begins. The only thing resembling suspense is the question of which of Count Barby's daughters he will choose. At stake in his marriage is not the personal fulfillment so central to most nineteenth-century novels, but rather the fulfillment of generations to come; his is not a personal but a symbolic act.

Charm and wit make Melusine the obvious candidate. She is, however, an enigmatic figure, associated with the fairy-tale creature, half-naiad, half-temptress, that charmed Fontane throughout his life. Equivocal allusions regarding her first marriage, a legacy perhaps of the mythical figure after whom she is named, seem to imply repressed sexuality. Indeed, it has been suggested by Brüggemann that her humanitarianism may be a form of sublimation.[8] Her mysterious affinity to Lake Stechlin and the enigmatic phenomena associated with it, especially the red cockerel that arises from its turbulence to sound its warning throughout the countryside, is also implicit in her name and nature. Thus it is she who is closest to the lake's symbolic connotations and who presents its most unambiguous interpretation. To her falls the final message of the work, "It is not necessary that the Stechlins live on, but long live the Stechlin" (HF I/5, 388). Despite ambiguity, the implication is clear that while no institution or caste need endure forever, what must survive is the spirit of "the Stechlins," both in the humanity of Dubslav and in the intuitive awareness of the interrelatedness of all things expressed by the symbolism of Lake Stechlin.

That Armgard, someone specifically designated as a "silent type" (HF I/5, 155), should be chosen for Woldemar's bride would seem extraordinary for an author like Fontane. Her talents certainly do not lie in the give-and-take of witty conversation for which his characters are famous. But then it is not noncommittal social intercourse, the province of the rich and idle, but conscious commitment to social justice that is set as the goal of Fontane's "political" novel. In taking Elizabeth of Thuringia as her exemplar, in dedicating her life to others, Armgard establishes the ideal that the writer postulates for the new aristocracy of deed of the twentieth century, an aristocracy not necessarily with a "von" before its name but "a nobility from which the world really has something, *role models* for the modern age (because that's the nobility's real obligation) who intellectually and morally advance the world and don't go looking for their life's fulfillment in the egoistic laying up of dead things."[9] It is a tragedy of German history that Fontane's vision was to be light-years from the reality that ensued.

If Armgard represents the last best hope of the nobility, the concrete application of these principles to the Germany of the last decade of the nineteenth century is also a function of a new and practically engaged clergy, as represented by Pastor Lorenzen. In his interest in doctrines similar to those of the court preacher Adolf Stöcker (1835–1909) and in a form of socialism based on a Christianity not directly associated with established orthodox German Protestantism, Fontane alludes to sociopolitical forces abroad in the Reich as the century drew to its close. To what extent the nonbeliever actually supported them himself is not clear. Letters written at the time of *Der Stechlin,* while confirming his belief in the necessity for a change in the role of the aristocracy, nowhere avow the ideology put forward by Stöcker, although it is evident that his sympathies lay more and more in the direction of the lower classes. Moreover, Lorenzen specifically distances himself from Stöcker's national crusade, preferring a more modest range—"to dig a well, just at the spot where one stands" (HF I/5, 31)—suggesting that it is not so much political agitation, for that was what Stöcker's movement was as well, as a practical and selfless individual altruism that is ultimately needed.

Not Stöcker but the Portuguese poet-pedagogue João de Deus, whose obituary Fontane drew on, becomes the lodestar of the novel's central idea: a new egalitarianism grounded in Christian values, derived not from the petrified tenets of hidebound ecclesiastical establishments (parodied in personalities such as Adelheid and the careerist Koselegger) but rather from the Sermon on the Mount and Paul's first Epistle to the Corinthians. Significantly, it is Lorenzen, as cited by Woldemar, who diagnoses the primary problem of the aristocratic-bourgeois social order of the Reich and postulates its solution: "Our entire society (and particularly nowadays, that which specifically refers to itself as such) is built on the ego. That is its curse and that is what is inevitably going to destroy it. The Ten Commandments, that was the Old Covenant; but the New Covenant has a different one, a single commandment, and that resounds in the words: 'And if there is not love . . .'" (HF I/5, 158).

Thus, with the solemn salute to Lorenzen and his Portuguese model, through the crossing of arms between the agnostic Melusine and the Catholic Baroness Berchtesgaden, as well as the altruistic Armgard and the nominally Lutheran Woldemar (HF I/5, 159), Fontane presages not only the relationship between the young Stechlin and Armgard but also the commitment by members of the Prussian ruling class to a new covenant that will transcend traditional affiliations.

Melusine and Lorenzen in chapter 29 present Fontane's concerns for the future of Germany if the anachronistic socioeconomic structure of the Reich continues. Requesting Lorenzen's support for Woldemar, her brother-in-law-to-be, in whom she sees the potential not only for enlightened leadership but also for conservative intransigence, Melusine now manifests her function as prophetess. Her unwillingness to have the snow removed from the surface of the lake derives from her duality as a realistic figure and an allegorical one. As the former, she is aristocrat enough not to disturb the status quo by releasing forces of change she knows will emerge soon enough. Moreover, she is inherently a figure whose concerns are with an age yet to come and who—like the author himself—can advise and warn but do little to effect change. Yet in the book's most significant passage, she reveals to Lorenzen its primary message: "I respect that which is. At the same time, of course, that which is emerging too, for the very thing that is emerging will sooner or later itself be that which is. As far as it deserves it, we should love everything old, but it's for the new that we really should live. And above all, as the Stechlin teaches us, we should never forget the great interrelatedness of things. To cut one's self off means to wall one's self in, and to wall one's self in is death" (HF I/5, 270).

Thus, although it is Melusine who expresses the enduringly valid principles on which *Der Stechlin* is based, it is to a new nobility, as exemplified by Waldemar and Armgard, and to a rededicated clergy, as personified in Lorenzen, that their practical application in the German Reich falls. Through them the political aspects of Fontane's novel are most clearly delineated. In a brief digression during the conversation between Melusine and Lorenzen, the latter explicates the historical situation. Hindering the Reich's progress into the twentieth century have been the inflexibility of an ossified state Lutheran church, which Lorenzen differentiates from true Christianity, and the aristocracy, with its "naive inclination to consider everything 'Prussian' as a higher cultural form" (HF I/5, 271). Lorenzen-Fontane concedes that Hohenzollern Prussia had three great past epochs during which the nobility played a leading role. But just as the monument to the heroes of Cremmer Damm is no longer visible in the evening darkness, the era of valiant deeds by an agrarian-based military caste has also faded, and the prosaic age of inventors and discoverers has begun. The Wilhelmine Reich's efforts to preserve a petrified neofeudalistic social order contravene the course of history, and the desire of its traditional first families for self-preservation, in the belief that "things won't be able to go on without them," is decried as being out of step with the march of the times:

Things surely will go on without them. They're no longer the pillars that hold everything up, they're the old stone and moss roof that unquestionably goes on weighing and pushing down but that can't protect us against storm any more. It may well be that the aristocratic days will come back some time, but right now wherever we look we stand under the sign of a democratic worldview. A new age is dawning. I think a better and happier one. And if not a happier one, then at least a time with more oxygen in the air, a time in which we can breathe better. And the more freely one breathes, the more one lives. (HF I/5, 274)

Fontane's letters, especially those to Georg Friedlaender, contain even more aggressive statements of the same views; in some cases, he actually calls for the elimination of the titled class. In the final words of the novel, although not going quite that far, Fontane makes it unmistakably clear that the future of Germany is tied not to the continued existence of the nobility but to the readiness to accept the forces of democratic change. The appearance of the child Agnes in her red stockings as the elder Stechlin lies dying makes symbolically evident his thoughts about what is likely to evolve.

Obviously *Der Stechlin* offers the hope that along with the orthodox Prussian state church the titled class would provide the political and cultural underpinnings for the coming era. This hope is implied by the marriage of the two protagonists of an enlightened nobility, Woldemar and Armgard. History, as we know now, would have it otherwise. If these two fictional proponents of a better aristocracy and a better Germany had lived to celebrate their golden anniversary, the year would have been 1947.

Conclusion

"The modern novel should be a picture of the age, of *its* age" (HF III/1, 319). Thus Fontane's succinct prescription in an essay from 1855, almost a quarter century before his first work in the genre, *L'Adultera,* was to appear. Applicable to a greater or lesser extent to every one of his novels dealing with the contemporary period, it is one of the main principles of his realism. We recollect his comment regarding *L'Adultera,* that it was the desire only to depict life as it was, without didactic tendency, that guided him. And yet, as has been noted, Fontane eschewed the mere piling up of fact upon fact. Although his works harbor a great mass of detail from which the reader can indeed gleen substantial information about daily life in the Second Reich, in almost every one of them underneath such detail lies a rich substructure of the transfiguring poetic-literary element, contained in the subtle interplay of characters, foreshadowing, symbolism and deftly employed leitmotivs. Along with this stands his undeniable superiority in the presentation of character—primarily through dialogue—a technique that more than with any German writer before Thomas Mann endowed his work with its timelessness and relative universality. Fontane's novels are above all novels of conversation, the give-and-take of personalities in a stately dance of social convention. Individuals reveal who they are and what they are through what they say. Rarely, especially as his fictional style matured, does the author intrude with personal comment.

Also at the basis of this highly subtle style was, as we have seen, Fontane's fascination with the psychology of the outsider, the individual who either by criminal or moral transgression violates the conventions of the society he rendered so deftly in his dialogue. It is chiefly women on whom he focused. With the exception of Schach, all his greatest figures are women, for it was especially through its female victims that he was able to delineate the failings of the essentially masculine-dominated upper class social and moral order of Bismarck's Reich. It was left to later writers such as Heinrich and Thomas Mann and Alfred Döblin to explore other social classes and other aspects of

German society. Nevertheless, they all owed something to Fontane; as their predecessor in the development of the realistic German novel he had no peer.

Yet relative neglect has been accorded Fontane in the non-German speaking world. Despite his stature as Germany's pre-eminent realist in the realm of the novel before Thomas Mann, he is rarely counted elsewhere among the leading contemporary writers of his age such as Flaubert, Zola, Tolstoy, Trollope, or Henry James. A recent dissertation, pointing out the extreme difficulty of dealing with an author of such conversational nuance and cultural chiaroscuro as Fontane, has placed part of the blame at the door of translators.[1] It is true. Fontane's subtleties and the cultural sophistication he demands of his readers do not allow him to be translated easily.

Yet this cannot be the entire story. Other factors, I believe, also play a role. Not the least is the cultural dimension. Not without reason, Fontane's world has been to a great extent discredited by history. As a result, Germanophobia and its consequences are easily discernible in Anglo-Saxon realms. The conscious extirpation of German culture in the United States following the 1914 invasion of Belgium and the sinking of the *Lusitania* two years later, not to mention the events of the Second World War and the Holocaust, tended to greatly diminish interest in the history—and literature—associated with the German language. This is especially the case for Prussia on which the stigma of unchecked militarism has weighed heavily. Despite his own scepticism towards the forces which engendered it, Fontane had been the victim of such cultural antipathy. Indeed, Anglo-Saxon disdain for Prussian armed adventure is documented by Fontane himself in scenes such as that in *Irrungen, Wirrungen* when Botho's wife relates how a Scottish acquaintance she has made while taking the cure bemusedly equates the achievements of one of Prussia's first soldiering families with those of his horse thief ancestors.

At the same time, despite his achievement for German letters, on the world literary stage Fontane must take a back seat to more dominant figures. It cannot be denied, that all of Fontane's works, as we have seen, with the exception of *Unwiederbringlich* and *Graf Petöfy,* deal with problems embedded preeminently in the Prussian character or in the social matrix of the Second Reich. That is their strength and at the same time their weakness. As documents of the era they will be read for as long as interest in the Second Reich survives—predominantly, however, only by those for whom the Second Reich is inherently of interest. Fontane was, as I have attempted to show, a consummate artist, but his range must be considered a local one that is not likely to garner international acclaim on the scale of a Tolstoy or Flaubert. That does not undermine his significance for the German novel or the history of the modern novel in general. Through Fontane the German novel left the realm of the idyllic and took significant strides towards the international importance which the next generation of German writers would achieve.

The Fontane renaissance has now ebbed. The number of publications devoted to him, which hit a high point in the 1970s, has gradually subsided although it has by no means ceased. Recent scholarship has tended to focus less on the fiction than on Fontane's literary and art criticism. A realm also awaiting fuller exploration is the author's lyric poetry. Yet although substantial work remains to be done in these areas for its own sake, its primary value lies in the light it throws on the novelist's technique and attitudes, for it is unquestionably on his fiction that Fontane's enduring and international fame securely rests.

Publication in recent decades of three extensive and substantially annotated sets of Fontane's works not only underscores his importance for German letters but makes the likelihood of a single critical edition of the complete works in the near future almost impossible. For English speaking readers, however, there remains the question of translations, above all of *Der Stechlin* and *Mathilde Möhring* and perhaps also of *Quitt*. It is to be hoped that these will become available before the centennial of the author's death in 1998.

In the years following the establishment of the German Democratic Republic, the primary center of Fontane studies was the *Theodor-Fontane-Archiv* of the German State Library in Potsdam. The archive served as a focal point of research, manuscript collection and preservation and twice yearly issued the *Fontane Blätter,* a periodical devoted to the publication of research, bibliography, and critical evaluation of works appearing on the author. In December 1990, however, following the reunification of Germany, a new organisation, the Fontane Gesellschaft (Fontane Society), was created in Potsdam. It is likely that the society will eventually become affiliated with the Fontane Archive and share common quarters with it, while also taking over publication of the *Fontane Blätter,* perhaps in the form of a yearbook. Its founding renews the hope that the center of Fontane research will continue to be

Conclusion

where it should be, in or near Theodor Fontane's city, Berlin, and that in the wake of German reunification the ease of access now assured to the Fontane Archive will, as the centenary of his death approaches, enable Fontane scholarship to flourish.

Notes and References

Chapter One

1. S. S. Prawer, "Catching the Tone. Theodor Fontane, *The Woman Taken in Adultery* and *The Poggenpuhl Family*," Times Literary Supplement, 30 November 1979, 58.
2. Thomas Mann, "Der alte Fontane." In *Gesammelte Werke* (Oldenburg: S. Fischer Verlag, 1960), vol. 9, 23.
3. Heinrich Mann, "Theodor Fontane, Gestorben vor 50 Jahren." 1948. Quoted by Hans Heinrich Reuter in, *Fontane* (Munich: Nymphenburger Verlagshandlung, 1968), 27; hereafter cited in the text as Reuter.
4. Theodor Fontane, *Werke, Schriften und Briefe*, 2d ed., Walter Keitel and Helmuth Nürnberger, eds., Abteilung III, *Aufsätze, Kritiken, Erinnerungen*, Volume 4, *Autobiographisches*, ed. Walter Keitel, (Munich: Carl Hanser Verlag: 1973), 18. As far as possible, all original quotations are translated from this edition of Fontane's works, often referred to as the "Hanser Ausgabe" or "Hanser Fontane," hereafter cited in the text with section, volume, and page number as HF. Particulars of the complete edition are as follows: Theodor Fontane, *Werke, Schriften und Briefe*, 2d ed., Walter Keitel and Helmuth Nürnberger, eds., Abteilung I, *Sämtliche Romane, Erzählungen, Gedichte und Nachgelassenes*, Walter Keitel and Helmuth Nürnberger, eds., 4 vols. (Munich, Carl Hanser Verlag: 1970). Abteilung II, *Wanderungen durch die Mark Brandenburg*, Walter Keitel and Helmuth Nürnberger, eds., 3 vols. (Munich: Carl Hanser, 1968). Abteilung III, *Aufsätze, Kritiken, Erinnerungen*, Jürgen Kolbe, Sigmar Gerndt, Helmuth Nürnberger, Heide Streiter-Buscher, Walter Keitel and Christian Andree, eds., 5 vols. (Munich: Carl Hanser, 1966). Abteilung IV, *Briefe*, Otto Drude, Helmuth Nürnberger, Gerhard Krause, Christian Andree, and Manfred Helge, eds., 5 vols. (Volume 5 in preparation) (Munich: Carl Hanser, 1962–).
5. Theodor Fontane to Bernhard von Lepel, 5 October 1849: HF IV/1, 86.
6. Fontane's statement in *Von zwanzig bis dreißig* (HF III/4, 183), that on the day of his examination he was even more cheered by the publication of his novella does not correspond to events. The examination took place in December 1839, some weeks before the story appeared in January 1840. By then several poems had also been printed in Berlin journals.
7. In *Von zwanzig bis dreißig*, the author erroneously recollects (HF III/4, 249) that it was with "Shakespeare's Strumpf" (Shakespeare's sock), a satire on the Leipzig Schiller Club's recent acquisition of a vest belonging to the

poet, that he had established connections with *Die Eisenbahn*. In fact, the poem appeared in the *Leipziger Tageblatt* in November 1841.

8. Details concerning the extent of members' radical activities are supplied by Christa Schultze in "Fontane und Wolfsohn. Unbekannte Materialien," *Fontane Blätter* 2, no. 3 (1970): 151–71 (Potsdam: Theodor-Fontane Archiv der Deutschen Staatsbibliothek), and "Fontane's 'Herwegh-Klub' und die studentische Progreßbewegung 1841/42 in Leipzig," *FB* 2, no. 5 (1971): 327–39.

9. Helmuth Nürnberger, *Der frühe Fontane: Politik. Poesie. Geschichte. 1840 bis 1860* (Hamburg: Christian Wegner Verlag, 1967), 301; hereafter cited in the text as Nürnberger.

10. Under this title the episode is recalled in detail as part of *A Summer in London* (HF III/I, 150ff.).

11. The exact date is unclear. See Wolfgang Paulsen, *Im Banne der Melusine. Theodor Fontane und sein Werk* (Bern, Frankfurt am Main, New York, Paris: Peter Lang, 1988), 8ff.

12. Fontane to Theodor Storm, 14 February 1854: HF IV/1, 376.

13. See Bange's study, which attempts to come to terms with the seeming discrepancy between Fontane's liberalism and conservatism. Pierre Bange, "Zwischen Mythos und Kritik Eine Skizze über Fontanes Entwicklung bis zu den Romanen," in *Fontane aus heutiger Sicht: Analysen und Interpretationen seines Werkes,* ed. Hugo Aust (Munich: Nymphenburger Verlangsbuchhandlung, 1980), 17–55.

14. Fontane did not favor a suggested reprinting of his first war book in 1894.

15. Fontane to Heinrich Jacobi, 23 January 1890: HF IV/4 18.

Chapter Two

1. Fontane to Paul Heyse, 9 December 1878: HF I/3, 758.
2. Fontane To Wilhelm Hertz, 8 January 1879: HF I/3, 759.
3. Fontane to Wilhelm Hertz, 24 November 1878: HF I/3, 755.
4. It has been shown by Walter Wagner that foreshadowing is the principal unifying structural element in the novel. Walter Wagner, *Die Technik der Vorausdeutung in Fontanes "Vor dem Sturm" und ihre Bedeutung im Zusammenhang des Werkes* (Marburg: Elwert, 1966).
5. Peter Demetz, *Formen des Realismus: Theodor Fontane* (Munich: Carl Hanser Verlag, 1964), 76; hereafter cited in the text as Demetz.

Chapter Three

1. So too was *Vor dem Sturm,* which on 29 January 1879 the critic Julius Rodenberg characterized as "a chain of ballads" (HF I/3, 761).
2. Fontane to Paul Lindau, 6 May 1878: HF IV/1, 877.

3. Fontane to Emilie Fontane, 11 August 1878. In *Theodor Fontane: Der Dichter über sein Werk*, ed. Richard Brinkmann with Waltraud Wiethölter (Munich: Deutscher Taschenbuch Verlag, 1977), II, 246.

4. Fontane to Wilhelm Hertz, 6 May 1878: HF IV/1, 877.

5. Some of Fontane's contemporaries, generally favorable to the work as a whole, also found the language problematic. See Frederick Betz, *Theodor Fontane: Grete Minde Erläuterungen und Dokumente* (Stuttgart: Philipp Reclam jun., 1986), 44–58.

6. Walter Müller-Seidel, *Theodor Fontane: Soziale Romankunst in Deutschland* (Stuttgart: J. B. Metzler, 1975), 74; hereafter cited in the text as Müller-Seidel.

7. Conrad Wandrey, *Theodor Fontane*, (Munich: C. H. Beck'sche Verlagsbuchhandlung, 1919), 147; hereafter cited in the text as Wandrey.

8. See, for instance, Klaus Globig, "Theodor Fontane 'Grete Minde': Psychologische Studie, Ausdruck des Historismus oder sozialpolitischer Appel?" *Fontane Blätter* 4, no. 8 (1981), Potsdam: 1981: 706–13. Responses by Volker Giel, Hans Ester, Jörg Thunecke and Joachim Biener are contained in *Fontane Blätter* 5, no. 1 (1982): 76–82.

9. See Adelheid Bosshart, *Theodor Fontanes historische Romane*, (Winterthur: Verlag P. G. Keller, 1957), 44.

10. See Eckart Pastor, "Das Hänflingsnest. Zu Theodor Fontanes *Grete Minde*." *Tidschrift voor levende Talen*, 44, (1978): 99–110.

11. Fontane to Wilhelm Hertz, 17 June 1866: HF I/3, 740.

12. See Hubert Ohl, "Theodor Fontane," in *Handbuch der deutschen Erzählung*, ed. Karl Konrad Pohlheim (Düsseldorf: Bagel, 1981), 346.

13. Annotated editions as well as studies such as Pierre-Paul Sagave, *Theodor Fontane: Schach von Wuthenow: Dichtung und Wirklichkeit* (Frankfurt am Main/ Berlin: Verlag Ulstein GmbH, 1966), hereafter cited in the text as Sagave, indicate the extent and thoroughness of Fontane's integration of original sources.

14. Fontane to Wilhelm Hertz: 17 June 1866: HF I/3, 740.

15. See H. Rudolf Vaget, "Schach in Wuthenow: 'Psychographie' und 'Spiegelung' im 14. Kapitel von Fontanes 'Schach von Wuthenow.'" *Monatshefte* 61 (1969): 1–14.

Chapter Four

1. Werner Hoffmeister, "Theodor Fontanes 'Mathilde Möhring' Milieustudie oder Gesellschaftsroman?" *Zeitschrift für deutsche Philologie* 92 (1973), 128.

2. See Henry Garland, *The Berlin Novels of Theodor Fontane* (Oxford: Clarendon Press, 1980), 2ff.

3. Fontane to Joseph Viktor Widmann, 27 April 1894: HF I/2, 836.

4. Fontane to Martha Fontane, 5 May 1883: HF I/2, 834.

5. Fontane to Paul Pollack, 10 February 1891: HF I/2, 835.
6. See Heide Eilert, "Im Treibhaus: Motive der europäischen Décadence in Theodor Fontanes Roman 'L'Adultera'," *Jahrbuch der deutschen Schillergesellschaft* 22 (1978): 496–517.
7. Fontane to Adolf Glaser, 25 April 1885: HF I/2, 871.
8. Fontane to Paul Schlentner, 2 June 1887: HF I/2, 873.
9. Fritz Martini, *Deutsche Literatur im bürgerlichen Realismus, 1848–1893*, 3d ed. (Stuttgart: J. B. Metzlersche Verlagsbuchhandlung, 1974), 773: hereafter cited in the text as Martini.
10. Fontane to Mathilde von Rohr, 19 April 1887: HF I/2, 872.
11. Helmuth Nürnberger, *Theodor Fontane in Selbstzeugnissen und Bilddokumenten* (Reinbeck bei Hamburg: Rowohlt Taschenbuch Verlag GmbH, 1968), 138; hereafter cited the in text as Nürnberger, *TF in Selbstzeugnissen*.
12. Indeed, the picture it presented was so accurate that shortly after its publication the author was visited by a nearly hysterical woman claiming— to his consternation—that it was her story he had told. Fontane to Paul Schlenther, 20 September 1887: HF I/2, 918.
13. Fontane to Emil Dominik, 14 July 1887: HF I/2, 913. This statement, incidentally, set off a veritable frenzy of what has been referred to as interpretive safaris. See Karl S. Guthke, "Fontanes 'Finessen' 'Kunst' oder 'Künstelei'?" *Jahrbuch der deutschen Schillergesellschaft* 26 (1982): 235–61.
14. Fontane to Emil Dominik, 14 July 1887 HF I/2, 913.
15. Reported by Wandrey (Wandrey, 213) as having been addressed to the editor of the *Vossische Zeitung*.
16. Fontane to Theodor Fontane, 8 September 1887: HF I/2, 917.
17. As in most Fontane novels, names play an important part. The name Lene is particularly plebeian, and also a contraction of Magdalene, the penitent. Yet Lene, although certainly the former, is by no means the latter. Similarly, Botho's name is associated only with the Prussian aristocracy and obscure in its origins, especially to Frau Dörr, whose physical attributes certainly belie the connotations of her marital name, associated with the word *dürr:* skinny or scrawny. On name symbolism, see Demetz, 193–203.
18. Dirk Mende, "Dann lebt man ohne Glück": Epilogue to Theodor Fontane, *Irrungen, Wirrungen* (Munich: Wilhelm Goldmann Verlag, 1980), 177.
19. An excellent study of the relationship of the two halves of the novel to one another is F. M. Subiotto, "The Use of Memory in Fontane's *Irrungen, Wirrungen*," pp. 478–89 in *Formen realistischer Erzählkunst. Charlotte Jolles in Honour of her 70th Birthday.* Ed. Jörg Thunecke (Nottingham: 1979).
20. Fontane to Friedrich Stephany, 16 July 1887 HF I/2, 914.
21. It has been argued, in fact, that Fontane's employment of the leitmotiv was derived from his study of Wagner's theoretical prose, a position generally denied today on the premise that the leitmotiv was as much a literary

device as a musical one and indeed probably originated with literary sources. See Dieter Borchmeyer, *Das Theater Richard Wagners: Idee—Dichtung—Wirkung* (Stuttgart: Phillip Reclam jun., 1982), 316ff.

22. Fontane to Emil Dominik, 3 January 1888: HF I/2, 954.
23. Fontane to Theodor Wolff, 28 April 1890: HF I/2, 924.
24. Fontane to Theodor Wolff, 24 May 1890: HF I/2, 959.
25. The source is a favorite of Fontane's, Holtei's operetta *Der alte Feldherr*, also used for a song occurring with equal symbolic significance in *Irrungen, Wirrungen*. See Liselotte Voss, *Literarische Präfiguration dargestellter Wirklichkeit bei Fontane: Zur Zitatstruktur seines Romanwerks* (Munich: Wilhelm Fink Verlag, 1985), 185ff.
26. Fontane to Paul Schlentner, 13 June 1888: HF I/2 955.
27. Fontane to Theodor Fontane, jr., 9 May 1888: HF I/4, 776.
28. See David Turner, "Fontane's Frau Jenny Treibel: A Study in Ironic Discrepancy," *Forum for Modern Language Studies* 8, no. 2 (1972): 132–47.
29. Dieter Kafitz, "Die Kritik am Bildungsbürgertum in 'Frau Jenny Treibel,'" *Zeitschrift für deutsche Philologie*, 91 (1973): 74–101; hereafter cited in text as Kafitz.
30. David Turner, "Coffee or Milk?—That is the Question: On An Incident From Fontane's *Frau Jenny Treibel*," *German Life and Letters* 21 (1967–68): 330–35.
31. Originally in Theodor Fontane, *Romane und Erzählungen,* ed. Gotthard Erler, Antita Golz and Jürgen Jahn, 8 vols. (Berlin and Weimar: Aufbau Verlag, 1969–). This edition, known as the "Aufbau Ausgabe," is hereafter cited in the text as AA.
32. Theodor Fontane, *Mathilde Möhring.* Auf Grund der Handschrift herausgegeben von Gotthard Erler. (Munich: 1971), Anmerkung 1, p 127. Cited in Günther Mahal, "Fontanes *Mathilde Möhring,*" *Euphorion* 69 (1975):127; hereafter cited in text as Mahal.
33. It may be noted that in a sketch for chapter 10, not integrated into the manuscript, Fontane has Mathilde say, "I'll take care of seeing to it that he gets to be something. People are saying there's money just lying in the streets. You only have to have eyes in your head and look for it. . . . Why for the right person it's all over the place. Anyways, he's a good-looking fellow and almost looks like one a th'postles. I'll bring him along. My name isn't Tilde if we don't have a wedding on St. John's Day" (HF I/4, 856).
34. See Ingrid Mittenzwei, *Die Sprache als Thema: Untersuchungen zu Fontanes Gesellschaftsromanen* (Bad Homburg, Berlin, Zurich: Verlag Gehlen, 1970) 133ff; Demetz, 177; Hartmut Reinhardt; "Die Wahrheit des Sentimentalen," *Wirkendes Wort* 29 (1979): 318ff.
35. Details of the Ardenne affair were rediscovered and published by H. W. Seiffert with Christel Laufer in "Fontanes 'Effi Briest' und Spielhagens 'Zum Zeitvertreib': Zeugnisse und Materialien," pp. 255–300 in Hans Wer-

ner Seiffert, *Studien zur neueren deutschen Literatur* (Berlin: Akademie-Verlag, 1964).

36. Fontane to Friedrich Spielhagen, 21 February 1896: HF I/4 711.

37. Anna Marie Gilbert, "A New Look at *Effi Briest:* Genesis and Interpretation," *Deutsche Vierteljahresschrift für Literaturwissenschaft und Geistesgeschichte* 53 (1979): 96–114.

38. Peter-Klaus Schuster, *Theodor Fontane: Effi Briest—Ein Leben nach christlichen Bildern* (Tübingen: Max Niemeyer Verlag, 1978).

39. See Wolfgang Paulsen, "Zum heutigen Stand der Fontane Forschung," *Jahrbuch der deutschen Schillergesellschaft* 25 (1981): 485, for recent conjectures on the origin of the name Effi.

40. See Reinhard H. Thum, "Symbol, Motif and Leitmotif in Fontane's *Effi Briest*," *Germanic Review* 54 (1979): 118. The subject is also thoroughly discussed by Demetz, 204ff.

41. Gertrude Tax-Schulze, "Andeutung und Leitmotiv in Fontane's 'Effi Briest,'" *Fontane Blätter* 3, (1970): 517.

42. J. P. Stern, *Reinterpretations* (New York: Basic Books, 1964), 319.

Chapter Five

1. As Brinkmann points out, nature for its own sake scarcely exists in Fontane's work. Richard Brinkmann, *Theodor Fontane: Über die Verbindlichkeit des Unverbindlichen.* 2d ed. (Tübingen: Max Niemeyer Verlag, 1977), 21.

2. Cf. Demetz, 164.

3. Hans Friedrich Rosenfeld, *Zur Entstehung Fontanischer Romane,* (Groningen, Den Haag: 1926), quoted in HF I/2, 978.

4. Wolfgang Paulsen, "Zum Stand der heutigen Fontane-Forschung," *Jahrbuch der deutschen Schillergesellschaft* 25 (1981): 486.

5. Critical agreement on the historical-political background of the novel, apart from its use as a means of character presentation, is by no means unanimous. Demetz (Demetz, 165) holds that the novel is "without historical ballast and political burden." Others maintain various intermediate positions of disagreement. See HF I/2, 983. For an interpretation of political aspects of the novel, see Stefan Blessing, "*Unwiederbringlich*—ein historisch-politischer Roman? Bemerkungen zu Fontanes Symbolkunst," *Deutsche Vierteljahresschrift* 48 (1974), 672–703.

6. Fontane to Julius Rodenberg, 19 November 1890: HF I/2, 993.

7. Heide Eilert, "'Und mehr noch fast, wer liebt.' Theodor Fontanes Roman *Unwiederbringlich* und die viktorianische Sexualmoral," *Zeitschrift für deutsche Philologie* 101 (1982), 553; hereafter cited in the text.

8. As Gertrud M. Sakrawa and others have pointed out, Fontane was no friend of extremism in any form, and especially in religious matters. Another work on this problem, *Storch von Adebar,* which remained, however, a fragment, probably contributed to the final characterization of Christine.

See Gertrud M. Sakrawa, "Scharmanter Egoismus: Theodor Fontanes 'Unwiederbringlich,'" *Monatshefte* 61 (1969): 15–29.

9. For the significance of letters in *Unwiederbringlich* see Frances M. Subiotto, "The Function of Letters in Fontanes 'Unwiederbringlich,'" *Modern Language Review* 65 (1970), 308–18.

Chapter Six

1. Hubert Ohl, "Theodor Fontane," *Handbuch der deutschen Erzählung*, ed. Karl Konrad Polheim (Düsseldorf: August Bagel Verlag, 1981), 341.
2. Fontane to Georg Friedlaender, 16 November 1885: HF I/1 941.
3. See A. J. F. Ziegelschmid, "Truth and Fiction and Mennonites in the Second Part of Theodor Fontane's Novel 'Quitt': The Indian Territory," *The Mennonite Quarterly Review* 16 (October 4, 1942): 223–46.

Chapter Seven

1. Fontane to Georg Friedlaender, 3 April 1887: HF IV/3, 531.
2. On anti-Semitism in Fontane's life and works, see Reuter, 742–56 and Wolfgang Paulsen, "Theodor Fontane: The Philosemitic Antisemite," *Yearbook of the Leo Baeck Institute* 26 (1981): 303–22.
3. Fontane to Friedrich Spielhagen, 24 November 1896: HF I/4, 824.
4. Fontane to Siegmund Schott, 14 February 1897: HF I/4, 825.
5. Quoted in Eda Sagarra, *Theodor Fontane "Der Stechlin"* (München: W. Fink Verlag, 1986), 17; hereafter cited in text as Sagarra.
6. Fontane to Adolf Hoffmann, May/June 1897 (draft): HF I/5, 420.
7. Fontane to Adolf Hoffmann, May/June 1897 (draft): HF I/5, 420.
8. See Diethelm Brüggemann, "Fontanes Allegorien," *Neue Rundschau* 82, (1971): 500.
9. Fontane to Georg Friedlaender, 8 July 1895: HF IV/4, 459.

Conclusion

1. Edith H. Krause, *Theodor Fontane: Eine Rezeptionsgeschichtliche und Übersetzungskritische Untersuchung*, Ph.D. diss., New York University, 1987.

Selected Bibliography

The bibliography on Fontane is extensive. The following are some important studies, although articles mentioned in the notes are for the most part omitted. Instead I have chosen to offer translations and a selection of a few books and articles in English.

PRIMARY WORKS

In German

Sämtliche Werke. Edited by Edgar Groß, Kurt Schreinert, Rainer Bachmann, Charlotte Jolles, Jutta Neuendorff-Fürstenau, and Peter Bramböck. 24 vols.: Abteilung I, *Das gesamte erzählende Werk.* 8 vols.; Abteilung II, *Wanderungen durch die Mark Brandenburg.* 6 vols.; Abteilung III, *Meine Kinderjahre, Christian Friedrich Scherenberg und das literarische Berlin, Von Zwanzig bis Dreißig, Kriegsgefangen, Aus den Tagen der Okkupation, Aus England und Schottland, Unterwegs und wieder daheim, Politik und Geschichte, Balladen und Gedichte, Literarische Essays und Studien, Causerien über Theater, Aufsätze zur bildenden Kunst, Fragmente und frühe Erzählungen. Nachträge.* 10 vols. Munich: Nymphenburger Verlagshandlung, 1959–75. "Nymphenburger Ausgabe."

Werke, Schriften und Briefe. Abteilung I, *Sämtliche Romane, Erzählungen, Gedichte, Nachgelassenes.* Edited by W. Keitel, H. Nürnberger and Gotthard Erler, 2d ed. 4 vols. Munich: Carl Hanser Verlag, 1970. Abteilung II, *Wanderungen durch die Mark Brandenburg.* Edited by Walter Keitel and Helmut Nürnberger. Notes by Jutta Neuendorff-Fürstenau. 3 vols. Munich: Carl Hanser Verlag, 1968. Abteilung III, *Erinnerungen, Ausgewählte Schriften und Kritiken.* Edited by Jürgen Kolbe, Sigmar Gerndt, Helmuth Nürnberger, Heide Streiter-Buscher, Walter Keitel, and Christian Andree. 5 vols. Abteilung IV, *Briefe.* Edited by Otto Drude, Helmuth Nürnberger, Gerhard Krause, Christian Andree, and Manfred Helge. 5 vols. Volume 5 in preparation. Carl Hanser Verlag, 1966. "Hanser Ausgabe."

Romane und Erzählungen. Edited by Peter Goldammer, Gotthard Erler, Anita Golz, and Jürgen Jahn. 8 vols., Berlin and Weimar: Aufbau Verlag, 1969. Abteilung II, *Wanderungen durch die Mark Brandenburg.* Edited by Gotthard Erler and Rudolf Mingau, 6 vols. Berlin and Weimar: Aufbau

Verlag, 1976–. Abteilung III, *Autobiographische Schriften. Meine Kinderjahre, Von Zwanzig bis Dreißig, Scherenberg, Tunnelprotokolle, Autobiographische Aufzeichnungen aus dem Nachlaß, Kleine Autobigraphische Dokumente.* Edited by Gotthard Erler, Peter Goldammer, and Joachim Krueger. 3 vols. Berlin and Weimar (1982). Abteilung IV, Sämtliche Gedichte. 2 vols. In preparation.

B. *Translations of the Novels and Important Non-Fiction*

Across the Tweed. A Tour of Mid-Victorian Scotland. (Jenseits des Tweed). Translated by Brian Battershaw. London: Phoenix House, 1965.

Before the Storm. A Novel of the Winter of 1812–13. *(Vor dem Sturm).* Translated and edited with an introduction by R. J. Hollingdale. Oxford and New York: Oxford University Press, 1985.

Beyond Recall. (Unwiederbringlich). Translated with an introduction by Douglas Parmée. London and New York: Oxford University Press, 1964.

Delusions, Confusions. (Irrungen, Wirrungen). Translated with an introduction and notes by William L. Zwiebel. *The German Library,* Vol. 47. General Editor. Volkmar Sander. Editor, Peter Demetz. Foreword by J. P. Stern. New York: Continuum, 1989.

Effi Briest. Translated with an introduction by Douglas Parmée. Harmondsworth, Middlesex: Penguin Books, 1967.

Jenny Treibel. (Frau Jenny Treibel). Translated with introduction and notes by Ulf Zimmermann. New York: Ungar, 1976. Also contained in *The German Library,* Vol. 46.

Journeys to England in Victoria's Early Days. (Aus England). Translated by Dorothy Harrison. London: Massie, 1939.

L'Adultera. Translated by Lynn R. Eliason. New York: Peter Lang, 1990.

A Man of Honor. (Schach von Wuthenow). Translated with introduction and notes by E. M. Valk. New York: Ungar, 1975. Also contained in *The German Library,* Vol. 46. Foreword by Peter Gay. New York: Continuum, 1982.

The Poggenpuhl Family. (Die Poggenpuhls). Translated with notes by Gabriele Annan. Introduction by Erich Heller. Chicago and London: University of Chicago Press, 1979. Also contained in *The German Library,* Vol. 47. Foreword by J. P. Stern; introduction by William L. Zwiebel. New York: Continuum, 1989.

"The Social Status of the Writer." ("Die gesellschaftliche Stellung der Schriftsteller"). Translated by E. M. Valk. In *Formen realistischer Erzählkunst.* Nottingham: Sherwood Press Agencies, 1979.

Stine. Translated by Harry Steinhauer. Pages 321–96 in *Twelve German Novellas.* Edited by H. Steinhauer. Berkeley, Los Angeles, London: University of California Press, 1977.

A Suitable Match. (Irrungen, Wirrungen). Translated by Sandra Morris. London and Glasgow: Blackie, 1968.

"A Woman in My Years." ("Eine Frau in meinen Jahren"). Translated by Harry Steinhauer. Pages 272–87 in *Deutsche Erzählungen—German Stories: A Bilingual Anthology.* Edited by Harry Steinhauer. Berkeley, Los Angeles, London: University of California Press, 1984.

The Woman Taken in Adultery. (L'Adultera). Translated with notes by Gabriele Annan. With an introduction by Erich Heller. Chicago and London: University of Chicago Press, 1979.

SECONDARY WORKS

Books and Parts of Books

Attwood, Kenneth. *Fontane und das Preußentum.* Berlin: Haude und Spenersche Verlagsbuchhandlung, 1970.

Aust, Hugo. *Theodor Fontane: "Verklärung." Eine Untersuchung zum Ideengehalt seiner Werke.* Bonn: Bouvier Verlag Herbert Grundmann, 1974. A study of the ideational essence of Fontane's depiction of reality through an interpretation of selected works.

Aust, Hugo. Editor. *Fontane aus heutiger Sicht.* Munich: Nymphenburger Verlagshandlung, 1980. Broad and important collection of essays on various aspects of Fontane's works and life from the decade of the 1970s.

Bance, Alan F. *Theodor Fontane: The Major Novels.* Cambridge: Cambridge University Press, 1982. Presumes a good knowledge of the works. The best study in English.

Berman, Russell A. "The Dissolution of Meaning: Theodor Fontane." Pages 134–60 in *The Rise of the Modern German Novel: Crisis and Charisma.* Cambridge, Mass. and London, England: Harvard University Press, 1986. Deals primarily with *Irrungen, Wirrungen.*

Brinkmann, Richard. *Theodor Fontane: Über die Verbindlichkeit des Unverbindlichen.* Munich: Piper, 1967. Studies aspects of Fontane's realism.

Demetz, Peter. *Formen des Realismus: Theodor Fontane.* Munich: Hanser, 1964. An important study that traces Fontane's place in the tradition of European literary realism and analyzes his technique.

Garland, Henry B. *The Berlin Novels of Theodor Fontane.* Oxford: Clarendon Press, 1980. Offers clear, thoughtful, and sensitive interpretations.

Jolles, Charlotte. *Theodor Fontane.* 3d ed. Stuttgart: Metzler, 1983. An indispensable German bibliographical reference work.

———. "'Gideon ist besser als Botho.' Zur Struktur des Erzählschlusses bei Fontane." Pages 76–93. In *Festschrift für Werner Neuse,* Berlin: 1967. Analyzes with great deftness Fontane's technique of closure.

McHaffie, Margaret A. "Fontane's *Irrungen, Wirrungen* and the Novel of Realism." Pages 167–89 in *Periods in German Literature,* Vol. II, Edited by

J. M. Ritchie. London: Oswald Wolff, 1969. A study of *Irrungen, Wirrungen* as a novel of enhanced reality in the fashion practiced by Fontane and other German realists.

Martini, Fritz. *Deutsche Literatur im bürgerlichen Realismus 1848–1898*. 2d ed., Stuttgart: Metzler, 1964. A good overview of Fontane's fiction.

Müller-Seidl, Walter. *Theodor Fontane: Soziale Romankunst in Deutschland*. Stuttgart: Metzler, 1975. Explores in depth the sociological background of Fontane's literary development and works.

Nürnberger, Helmuth. *Der frühe Fontane: Politik, Poesie, Geschichte, 1840 bis 1860*. Hamburg: Wegner, 1967. 2d ed., Frankfurt a.M., Berlin, Vienna: Ullstein, 1975. A thorough study of Fontane's early years and works.

———. *Fontane in Selbstbildnissen und Bilddokumenten*. Reinbeck: Rowohlt, 1968. Excellent compact biographical introduction. A good starting point for readers of German. Contains an extensive bibliography.

Ohl, Hubert. "Theodor Fontane." Pages 339–55 in *Handbuch der deutschen Erzählung*. Edited by Karl Konrad Polheim. Düsseldorf: August Bagel Verlag, 1981. Covers the four criminal tales.

Pascal, Roy, "Theodor Fontane." Pages 178–214 in *The German Novel*. Oxford: Manchester University Press, 1956. A brief but insightful overview of "the most adult of the German novelists."

Paulsen, Wolfgang. *Im Banne der Melusine. Theodor Fontane und sein Werk*. Bern, Frankfurt a.M., New York, Paris: Peter Lang, 1988. An interpretation of Fontane's women figures based on a psycho-biography of the author and his friendship with Bernhard von Lepel.

Preisendanz, Wolfgang. Editor. *Theodor Fontane*. Darmstadt: Wissenschaftliche Buchgesellschaft, 1973. Contains articles by Thomas Mann, Georg Lukacs, and the older generation of German literary scholars.

Remak, Joachim. *The Gentle Critic: Theodor Fontane and German Politics 1848–1898*. Syracuse: Syracuse University Press, 1964. Fontane's political views of the Second Reich.

Reuter, Hans-Heinrich. *Fontane*. Munich: Nymphenburger Verlagshandlung, 1968. Sometimes hagiographic, occasionally ideological and formally confusing, nevertheless the best overall study of Fontane's life and works.

Robinson, A. R. *Theodor Fontane: An Introduction to the Man and his Work*. Cardiff: University of Wales Press, 1976. A good general introduction in English.

Sagarra, Eda. *Theodor Fontane: Der Stechlin: Text und Geschichte*. Munich: Fink, 1986. The sociopolitical background of Fontane's last novel.

Sasse, H. C. *Theodor Fontane. An Introduction to the Novels and Novellen*. Oxford: Blackwell, 1968.

Thunecke, Jörg, and Eda Sagarra. Editors. *Formen realistischer Erzählkunst. Festschrift für Charlotte Jolles*. Nottingham: Sherwood Press Agencies, 1979. A collection of essays and translations.

Wandrey, Conrad. *Theodor Fontane.* Munich: C. H. Beck'sche Verlagsbuchhandlung, 1919. The first important study and still worthy of consideration although now obsolete on many points.

Selected Articles in English

Avery, George C. "The Chinese Wall: Fontane's Psychograph of Effi Briest." Pages 18–38 in *Views and Reviews of Modern German Literature. Festschrift für Adolf D. Klarmann.* Edited by Karl S. Weimar. Munich: Delp, 1974.

Bance, Alan. F., "Fontane's 'Mathilde Möhring.'" *Modern Language Review* 69 (1974): 121–33. An astute close reading that seeks to justify the work's inclusion in the Fontane canon.

Greenberg, Valerie D. "The Resistance of *Effi Briest:* An (Un)told Tale," *PMLA* 103 (October 1988): 770–81. A feminist rereading of the novel's conclusion.

Guidry, Glenn A. "Myth and Ritual in Fontane's *Effi Briest.*" *Germanic Review* 59 (1984): 19–25. A mythopoetic study of leitmotiv, symbol, and social and mythic rituals in the novel.

Guthke, Karl S. "Fontane's Craft of Fiction: Art or Artifice?" Pages 67–94 in *Essays in Honor of James Edward Walsh.* Cambridge: The Goethe Institute of Boston and the Houghton Library, 1983. A critique of excesses of modern Fontane scholarship. Also in German in *Jahrbuch der deutschen Schillergesellschaft* 26 (1982): 235–61.

Kieffer, Bruce. "Fontane and Nietzsche: The Use and Abuse of History in *Schach von Wuthenow.*" *Germanic Review* 61 (1986): 29–35. Discusses similarities in both writers' criticism of Prussia and historicity.

Malcom, David. "A New View of Gideon Franke in Fontane's *Irrungen, Wirrungen.*" *New German Studies* 10 (1973): 45–53. Sees Franke as part of the newly conscious proletariat of the Second Reich.

Northcott, Kenneth. "Some Topoi in Fontane." *German Life and Letters* 38 (1984–85): 374–84. Deals with the function of windows and letters as semiotic devices in *Ellernklipp, Irrungen, Wirrungen,* and *Effi Briest.*

Rowley, Brian A. "Theodor Fontane: A German Novelist in the European Tradition?" *German Life and Letters* 15 (1961–62): 71–88. Although now historical, this article makes still valid points for Fontane's place in the canon of the European realistic novel.

Subiotto, Frances M. "Aspects of the Theatre in Fontane's Novels." *Forum for Modern Language Studies* 6 (1970): 149–68.

———. "The Ghost in *Effi Briest.*" *Forum for Modern Language Studies* 21 (1985): 137–50. A subtle interpretation of the problematic ghost as a symbol of forces absent in the relationships portrayed in the novel.

———. "The Use of Memory in Fontane's *Irrungen, Wirrungen.*" Pages 478–89 in *Formen realistischer Erzählkunst.* Nottingham: Sherwood Press Agencies, 1979. A sensitive study of the function of memory and memories as one of the primary constituents of the novel.

Index

Alexis, Willibald, 23
America, 109–10
Antiquarianism: and German culture, 29; in style, 31
Anti-Semitism, 62, 117
Ardenne, Armand Léon Baron von, 83–84
Ardenne, Elizabeth von, 83
Argo, 16, 22
Aristocracy: Fontane's attitude toward, 21, 112; caricatures of, 114–15, 122–23; decline of, 3, 62, 69, 112–27; future in Empire, 124, 126; ideal of, 6, 117; Junker, 62, 112; lifestyle of, 62, 96; military aristocracy (Schwertadel), 45, 113
Austen, Jane, 45

Ballad, 11, 12, 22; influence on prose, 25, 29, 34, 37, 100, 110
Baltic coast: in novels, 5, 46. *See also* Swinemünde
Berlin, 2, 7, 8, 40, 90, 119, 120; growth in nineteenth century, 3–4; character types, 65; milieu in Fontane's works, 2, 46, 49, 57, 58
Berliner Figaro, 8
Bismarck, Otto von, 1, 2; in Fontane's novels, 49, 62, 78, 81, 122
Bourgeoisie: Anglophilism of, 76; role in German Empire, 3; in Fontane's novels, 4, 8, 45, 75, 112; Fontane's disdain for, 72. *See also* German Empire
Brahm, Otto, 100
Brandenburg, 5, 22, 30, 46, 112, 119; in Fontane's works, 2
Brentano, Clemens: *Die Geschichte von dem braven Kasperl und dem schönen Annerl*, 37
Buddenbrooks (Mann), 2, 70
Burns, Robert, 82
Buska, Johanna, 90

Calvinism, 4; predestination, 26, 105, 110. *See also* Fatalism
Catholicism, 91, 92, 93, 104. *See also* Religion
Cornelius, Peter, 97

Daheim, 23, 113
Das Schloß am Meer (Uhland), 97
Decadence, 70
De Deus, Joao, 124
Demetz, Peter, 28, 33, 34, 35, 43, 52, 56, 94, 96, 100, 120
Der Kirchhof (Waiblinger), 98
Der Tod in Venedig (Mann), 70
Der Tunnel über der Spree, 11–12, 15, 16, 25, 29
Der 24. Februar (Werner), 37
Der Zauberberg (Mann), 70
Determinism, 35, 45
Deutscher Novellenschatz, 33
Deutschland, 67
Die Deutsche Rundschau, 71, 82, 95, 100, 119
Die Eisenbahn, 9
Die Gartenlaube, 77, 102, 103, 106, 111
Die Geschichte von dem braven Kasperl und dem schönen Annerl (Brentano), 37
Die Judenbuche (Droste-Hülshoff), 36
Die Jungfrau von Orleans (Schiller), 60
Die Kreuzzeitung (*Die neue Preußische Zeitung*), 17, 18, 22, 23
Die Leiden des jungen Werthers (Goethe), 70
Die Quitzows (von Wildenbruch), 116
Die Reise nach dem Glück (Heyse), 55–56
Die verhängnisvolle Gabel (Platen), 37
Die Wahlverwandtschaften (Goethe), 37, 50, 83, 97
Die Walküre (Wagner), 50
Die Weihe der Kraft (Werner), 42
Döblin, Alfred, 25, 128
Dominik, Emil, 53

145

Dos Passos, John, 25
Dresdener Zeitung, 14
Droste-Hüshoff, Die Judenbuche, 36

England: influence of, 17, 22; visits to, 10–11, 15, 16–17
English, translations from, 10
Erler, Gotthard, 77, 81
Ettlinger, Josef, 77
Eulenberg, Count Phillip zu, 53

Fatalism, 26, 36–37, 55, 84, 85, 105, 110. See also Religion
Faust (Goethe), 61
Flaubert, Gustav, 129
Fontane Archive, 130
Fontane, August, 7–8, 104
Fontane Blätter, 130
Fontane, Emilie Labry (mother), 2, 5
Fontane, Emilie Rouanet-Kummer (wife), 14, 71
Fontane, Friedrich, 67, 71, 82
Fontane, Georg, 116
Fontane Gesellschaft, 130
Fontane, Louis Henri, 4, 5, 10, 121
Fontane, Martha (Mete), 71
Fontane, Pierre Barthélemy, 4–5
Fontane scholarship, vii, 22, 130
Fontane, Theodor: as journalist, 14–19; as Prussian government correspondent, 14–17; as theater critic, 19; attitude toward novel, 128; early literary interests, 8–14; general content of novels; 4, military service, 10; neglect outside Germany, 129; reputation and stature, 1–2, 129; translations of works, vii–viii, 129, 130; view of role of fiction, 48; works on Prussian wars, 18, 23

WORKS
Allerlei Glück, 19, 30, 52
Als ich zwei dicke Bände herausgab, 21
Aus den Tagen der Okkupation, 18
Bilder und Briefe aus Schottland (Jenseits des Tweed), 18
Carl Stuart, 13
Cécile, 44, 52–57, 58, 87, 94

Der Stechlin, vii, 21, 46, 78, 112, 118–27
Die Likedeeler, 118
Die Poggenpuhls, 80, 112, 113–18, 119
Effi Briest, viii, 6, 21, 44, 82–89, 100, 113, 119
Ein Sommer in London, 15, 22
Ellernklipp, 29, 35–38, 110
Frau Jenny Treibel, 8, 24, 71–77, 100, 112
Geschwisterliebe, 8, 22
Graf Petöfy, 58, 90–95, 109, 129
Grete Minde, 29–35, 36, 47
Irrungen, Wirrungen, viii, 20, 44, 46, 57–66, 66, 67, 68, 69, 70, 71, 78, 87, 94, 100, 106, 129
James Monmouth, 16, 22
Jenseits des Tweed, 16, 18
Kiegsgefangen, 18
L'Adultera, 20, 45, 46–52, 75, 91, 95, 128
Mathilde Möhring, 77–82, 113
Meine Kinderjahre, 83, 113
Mönch und Ritter, 9
Preußenlieder, 13
Quitt, 102, 106–11
Schach von Wuthenow, 36, 38–44, 46, 47, 58, 87, 90, 91, 94, 99
Stine, 66–71, 78
Tuch und Locke, 16, 22
Unsere lyrische und epische Poesie seit 1848, 16
Unterm Birnbaum, 90, 102–5, 106, 110
Unwiederbringlich, 90, 95–101, 119, 129
Von Zwanzig bis Dreißig, 10, 13, 119
Vor dem Sturm, 12, 19, 22–28, 29, 30, 34, 37, 47, 104, 113, 117
Wanderungen durch die Mark Brandenburg, 1, 6, 12, 17, 18, 20, 23, 24, 25, 26, 30, 31, 53

Fontane, Theodor (son), 60
Franco-Prussian War, 67
Franzos, Karl Emil, 106

Index

Frederick the Great (king of Prussia), viii, 38, 42, 104
Freiligrath, Ferdinand, 9
Frey, Wilhelm, 106
Friedlaender, Georg, 21, 105, 112, 126
Friedrich, Gerhard, 70
Friedrich Wilhelm (electoral prince), 4
Friedrich Wilhelm I (king of Prussia), 87
Friedrich Wilhelm II (king of Prussia), 5
Friedrich Wilhelm III (king of Prussia), 5
Friedrich Wilhelm IV (king of Prussia), 9, 10, 97, 105

German Empire, 52, 57, 84, 106, 130; authoritarianism in, 107–9; Fontane's concerns for future of, 125–27; disillusionment with, 21; duelling in, 87–88; Fontane's significance for, viii, 1, 2, 129; militarism in, 27, 108; origins of, 2–4; place of women in, 55, 59–60, 85–86; values in, 48, 60, 64, 72, 78, 109, 128. *See also* Social classes
Germanophobia: influence on Fontane's reputation, 129
Goethe, Johann Wolfgang von, 1; *Faust* (Gretchen), 61; *Die Leiden des jungen Werthers*, 70; *Die Wahlverwandschaften* (*Elective Affinities*), 37, 50, 83, 97; *Wilhem Meisters Lehrjahre* (Mignon), 61, 66
Gutzkow, Karl, 8

Harz mountains, 35, 46
Hauptmann, Gerhart, 19
Heine, Heinrich, 9
Hertz, Wilhelm, 23, 30, 47, 53, 95, 106
Herwegh, Georg, 9; Herwegh Club, 12
Heyse, Paul, 24; *Deutscher Novellenschatz*, 33; *Die Reise nach dem Glück*, 55–56
Hoffmeister, Werner, 81
Hohenzollern: Prussian ruling family 2, 26, 126; Friedrich Wilhelm (electoral prince), 4; Frederick the Great (king of Prussia), viii, 38, 42, 104;

Friedrich Wilhelm I (king of Prussia), 87; Friedrich Wilhelm II (king of Prussia), 5; Friedrich Wilhelm III (king of prussia), 5; Friedrich Wilhelm IV (king of Prussia), 9, 10, 97, 105; Wilhelm I (German emperor), 3, 76, 84; Wilhelm II (German emperor), 21, 46, 78, 120
Howells, William Dean, 100
Huguenots, 4

Ibsen, Henrik, 19, 20, 100; *A Doll's House*, 51, 61; *Ghosts*, 20

James, Henry, 129
Junker class, 62, 112

Keyserling, Eduard von, 55
Kleist, Heinrich von 32, 102
Knobloch (poacher-murderer), 106
Kreuzzeitung. See *Die Kreuzzeitung*

L'Adultera (Tintoretto), 51
Laube, Heinrich, 8
Leitmotiv. See Literary devices
Lenau, Nikolaus, 8, 92
Lepel, Bernhard von, 11, 16, 95
Lindau, Paul, 109
Literary devices, 32, 34, 41–43, 55–56, 65–66, 77, 84–87, 88, 93–94, 98–99, 114, 123, 136n. *See also* Name symbolism
Lukacs, Georg, 56
Lutheranism, 97, in Prussia, 42, 43. *See also* Religion

Mahal, Günther, 81
Mahlzahn, Karl Hans von, 95
Manteuffel, Otto Freiherr von, 14
Mann, Heinrich, 2, 128
Mann, Thomas, 1, 2, 50, 70, 81, 83, 114, 128, 129; *Buddenbrooks*, 2, 70; *Der Tod in Venedig*, 70; *Der Zauberberg*, 70
Maria Stuart (Schiller), 110
Mark Brandenburg. See Brandenburg
Martini, Fritz, 55, 62, 94
Marwitz, August Ludwig von der, 26

Melusine. *See* Women: types
Meyer, Conrad Ferdinand, 100
Morality tales, 102–11
Morris, James, 21
Mozart, Wolfgang Amadeus: *The Magic Flute*, 68
Müller-Grote, 103
Müller-Seidel, Walter, 32, 34, 37, 55, 81, 105, 106
Mundt, Theodor, 8
Mythical traits: in *Effi Briest*, 85–87

Name symbolism, 64, 68, 76, 77, 99, 109, 114
Narrative style: conversational tone, 2, 31, 73, 128; structure, 24–25, 58, 68, 75, 84, 96, 99, 116–17, 118
Naturalism, 67, 78; Fontaine's attitude toward, 20
Neuruppin, 4, 5, 6, 7
Nietzsche, Friedrich, 49
Nobility. *See* Aristocracy
Nord und Süd, 46
Novalis (Hardenberg, Friedrich von), 70
Novel of high society, 54, 91, 95
Nürnberger, Helmuth, 17, 56, 106

Ohl, Hubert, 102

Parsifal (Wagner), 50
Paul, Saint: First Epistle to the Corinthians, 125
Paulsen, Wolfgang, 95
Percy, Bishop Thomas, 12
Platen, August Graf von, 8; *Die verhängnisvolle Gabel*, 37
Plotho, Elizabeth von, 83
Pole Poppenspaeler (Storm), 31
Prawer, S. S., 2
Predestination. *See* Fatalism
Preußische Zeitung, 15
Prince, John Critchley, 10
Proletariat: in novels. *See* Social classes
Prussia: and German Empire, 2–4; demoralization after 1806, 38; wars, 2

Prussian: character in Fontane's novels, 39, 40–41, 46, 79, 87, 90, 107–9, 129; militarism, 43, 97, 115, 129; provincialism, 122; state religion, 4. *See also* Brandenburg
Pseudohistoricism. *See* Antiquarianism
Psychology: in Fontane's fiction, 30, 35, 39, 71, 84, 91, 111, 128

Ravené, Louis, 47
Ravené, Therese, 47
Reich. *See* German Empire
Religion, 93, 125, 126; yearning for, 93
Revolution of 1848, 13
Rohr, Mathilde von, 38, 39
Romanticism, 25, 36–37, 100, 102–11. *See also* Fatalism

Sagarra, Eda, 120
Schack, Otto Ludwig Friedrich von, 38
Schiller, Friedrich, 70, 81; *Die Jungfrau von Orleans*, 60; *Maria Stuart*, 110; *Wallensteins Tod* (*Wallenstein's Death*), 54
Schnitzler, Arthur, 55
Schottländer, Salo, 47
Scott, Sir Walter, 12, 23
Second Reich. *See* German Empire
Silesia, 46, 106
Sermon on the Mount, 125
Social classes, 45; artists, 54; educated, 54, 74; lower, 74–75, 78. *See also* Aristocracy; Bourgeoisie
Sommerfeldt, Jenny, 71
Spielhagen, Friedrich, 118
Stifter, Adalbert, *Witiko*, 28
Stöcker, Adolf, 124
Storm, Theodor, 22; *Pole Poppenspaeler*, 31
Symbolism. *See* Literary devices
Swinemünde, 5, 84, 92
Szendro, Nickolaus Török von, 90

Ten Commandments, 125
Thackeray, William Makepeace, 15, 45; *Vanity Fair*, 15

Index

Tintoretto: *L'Adultera*, 51
Tolstoy, Leo, 27, 129; *War and Peace*, 27
Translations: of Fontane's works, vii–viii, 129, 130
Transfiguration, 128
Trollope, Anthony, 100, 129
Tunnel über der Spree, 11–12, 15, 16, 25, 29
Turgenev, Ivan, 100

Über Land und Meer, 90, 119
Uhland, Ludwig, *Das Schloß am Meer*, 97
Universum, 53

Vanity Fair (Thackeray), 15
Victorian sexual code, 98
Vom Fels zum Meer, 113
Vossische Zeitung, 18, 57, 59, 67; Fontane as theater critic for, 19, 20

Wagner, Richard, 49, 50, 66, 70, 95; *Die Walküre*, 50; *Parsifal*, 50

Waiblinger, Wilhelm: *Der Kirchhof*, 98
Wallensteins Tod (*Wallenstein's Death*) (Schiller), 54
Wandrey, Conrad, 33, 55, 94, 100, 117
War and Peace (Tolstoy), 27
Werner, Zacharias, *Der 24. Februar*, 37; *Die Weihe der Kraft*, 42
Westermanns Monatshefte, 36
Widmann, Joseph Viktor, 88
Wienbarg, Ludolf, 8
Wildenbruch, Ernst: *Die Quitzows*, 116
Wilhelm I (German emperor), 3, 76, 84
Wilhelm II (German emperor), 21, 46, 78, 120
Wilhelm Meisters Lehrjahre (Goethe), 61, 66
Witiko (Stifter), 28
Women: place in empire, 59, 85; types in Fontane's fiction, 37, 55, 79, 85, 128

Young Germany, 8

Zola, Emile, 100, 129

The Author

William L. Zwiebel is associate professor of German at The College of the Holy Cross in Worcester, Massachusetts. He completed his Ph.D. at the University of Pennsylvania in 1968 and studied at the Phillips Universität, Marburg an der Lahn, Germany. He has written on Adalbert Stifter and translated works by Fontane and Lessing for *The German Library,* published by Continuum.

He has received grants from the German Academic Exchange Service, the Goethe Institute, the Fulbright Commission, and the National Endowment for the Humanities.

The Editor

David O'Connell is professor of foreign languages and chair of the Department of Foreign Languages at Georgia State University. He received his Ph.D. from Princeton University in 1966, where he was a National Woodrow Wilson Fellow, the Bergen Fellow in Romance Languages, and a National Woodrow Wilson Dissertation Fellow. He is the author of *The Teachings of Saint Louis: A Critical Text* (1972), *Les Propos de Saint Louis* (1974), *Louis-Ferdinand Céline* (1976), *The Instructions of Saint Louis: A Critical Text* (1979), and *Michel de Saint Pierre: A Catholic Novelist at the Crossroads* (1990). He is the editor of *Catholic Writers in France Since 1945* (1983) and has served as review editor (1977–79) and managing editor (1987–90) of the *French Review*.